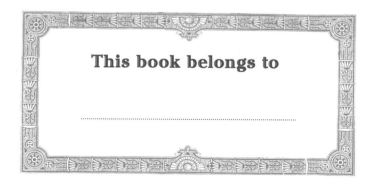

This book belongs to

....

She's Leaving Home

Monica Trápaga

LANTERN
an imprint of
PENGUIN BOOKS

This 'olla podrida' of tales and recipes
is dedicated with love to:

my Grandma Mary,
my mother, Margot,
my Manhattan mama, Janet Hoffman,
and most especially my daughter, Lil.

Contents

introduction

At some stage or another, a young girl has got to take that big step: steal her mother's copy of *The Cook's Companion*, smuggle out the well-seasoned Le Creuset casserole and set up house for herself.

In my case, it was a dog-eared scrapbook filled with page after crusty page of tried-and-true recipes, and a big black cast-iron frying pan. Luckily for me I came from a long line of good cooks and, as far back as I can remember, food and the ceremony that goes with it have always been fundamental to me.

The most important events in my life have been punctuated by food. In times of celebration, extravagant culinary concoctions and classic family favourites give the occasion meaning and purpose. In times of sadness, family companionship and the soft blanket of comfort food is the best rescue remedy. In times of adventure, the ways of the world are opened up via our tastebuds. They say money makes the world go round, but good food makes it worth spending.

My family is originally from the Philippines. My ancestors on my mother's side have Spanish and American roots, and on my father's side they are Spanish and Basque (a somewhat volatile combination!). My maternal grandfather, Luis Esteban, an actor and professional cartoonist, died the year before I was born, leaving his beautiful and elegant wife, Mary Case Esteban, as the head of the family.

Mary is now 101 years old, and still cooking. For almost fifty years she ran a successful catering business in Manila, cooking for state events, weddings, christenings and other celebrations. Her version of the traditional Filipino dish *bibingka malagkit* was so prized by then-president Ferdinand Marcos that he would send an armoured car round to her place to pick it up. She was also a couturier of note – responsible for the intricate embroidered décor in the home of the former president and his wife Imelda, along with many of their traditional outfits. Her name was synonymous with style, grace and truly amazing creations, whether in food or fashion.

My mother Margot's childhood under Grandma Mary's tutelage made her the adventurous gastronome she is today. As well as being an amazing and creative cook, Margot has the enthusiasm of Doris Day, the wardrobe of Jackie Onassis and the panache of Gina Lollobrigida. She also had the good sense to marry my father, Nestor Trápaga, a man with the spirit of Picasso, the smile of Omar Sharif and the thick black hair of Desi Arnaz. As a young couple they made a real splash on the Manila social scene and soon began a clan of their own. But life under the Marcos regime was not always easy, so after my siblings Ignatius, Luis Miguel and Rocio (Cio) were born, my parents started dreaming of alternative places to build their Camelot. That's how they came to move to Australia in 1963.

My family arrived here at a time when there were few ingredients in Australian pantries that were familiar to them: no chillies, garlic, saffron, eggplants or coriander. Parsley was only ever curly and used to garnish sausages in the butcher's window, and olive oil was found at the chemist, labelled 'For medicinal use only'. Margot's response to this was to plant a plethora of herbs and vegetables in the backyard that kept our neighbours fascinated, and the family and friends who dined at our place delighted.

I was born in 1965, an Aussie cockatoo amongst a flock of flamingos, although I looked more like a Mexican *chiquita*. I was doted on by my brothers and sister and indulged by my parents. At the age of four, I had my own kitchen (made out of a large packing crate) complete with a minia-ture saucepan set that fuelled my desire to cook. I was forever inviting family members and neighbours to sample my cooking: mudpies garnished with snail shells, corn-silk spaghetti with crabapple meatballs, and my famous peanut soup.

I'm sure I inherited my passion for cooking and entertaining from my mother, and she did everything possible to encourage this culinary love. She entertained in style and was unbelievably generous when it came to food. Her endless search for new and unusual ingredients took her well beyond the local supermarket. As a child, I remember her leaving the house at six in the morning to go to the Sydney fish markets (in those days, this was the only place you could get really fresh seafood). She'd bring home mysterious parcels tightly wrapped in butcher's paper and with a flamboyant flourish she'd tear them open – out would tumble kilos of fresh mussels, prawns, crabs and the occasional lobster. Our childhood parties were always extraordinary, with more costumes, games and party treats than Disneyland. This passion certainly seems genetic, as I see it now in my children – they adore food and will try anything.

Recently I married for the second time. My husband Simon, a wonderful, witty man, has four children of his own, so together we are the proud parents of six. Discovering each child's various culinary likes and dislikes has certainly been challenging. I am continually learning from them, and hopefully I've been able to instil in them a little of the love of food that the women in my life have passed on to me.

So why does someone with a great load of treasured family recipes want to write a cookbook and expose those well-guarded gems to the world? Well, two years ago my 21-year-old daughter Lil, part-time trapeze performer and full-time uni student, packed up her belongings (including a vast collection of hats and about two thousand books), and set up home on her own for the first time. She has entertaining in her bones – an insatiable appetite and an uncontrollable need to host. Nothing makes me happier than to receive a phone call from her requesting recipes, no matter how simple or difficult. I decided to create a volume of our favourite family recipes for her to take with her on her own life journey, a collection she could eventually add to herself and pass on to her own children.

These days, she is a qualified scientist and full-time trapeze performer, and although her calls are now often long-distance, things haven't changed much. Along with amusing letters and emails from remote corners of the world, I still get requests for recipes, but now I also get suggestions for previously un-thought-of culinary combinations and new exotic flavours. Lovely Lil is not just hosting dinner parties for a household anymore, she's cooking for a circus! She has sent me recipes from all over the world, prising gastronomic secrets from friends and acquaintances, and recalled many of our family's recipes that I'd forgotten.

So now this book, that started out as a gift from me to her, has become a gift for women everywhere. Young or old, there is nothing like cooking to bring people together. I've been fortunate to live with some great cooks in my life who have all graciously taught me a tip or two along the way. This book is nothing but a helping hand, a practical guide for those starting out, and most of all a way of passing on a little love.

Go forth with courage, roll up your sleeves, throw on your apron (and some good music), learn by your mistakes and try everything at least once. *Buon appetito!*

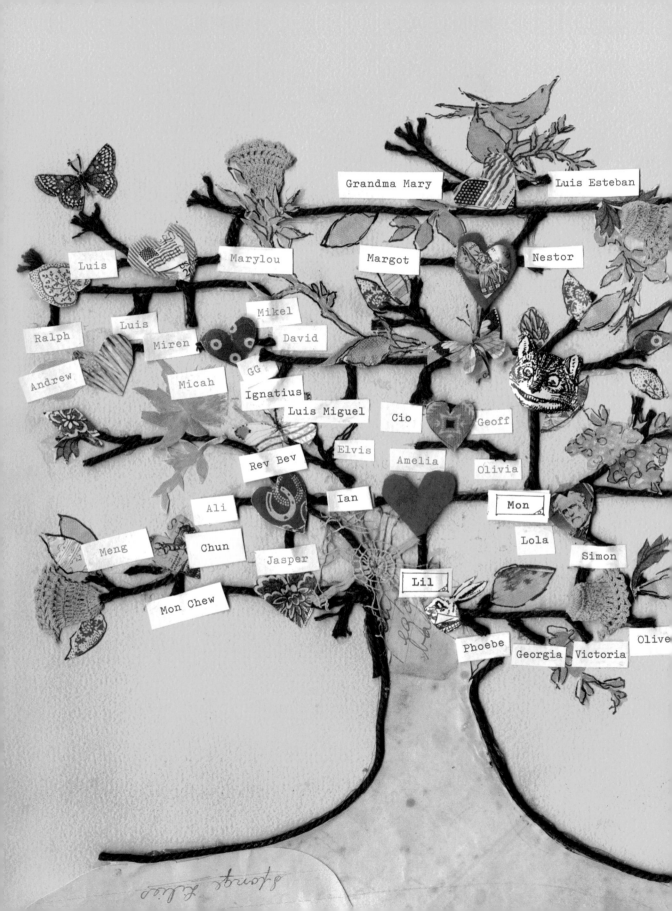

Luis

Jenny

Dino

Luis

Helen

Bianca

Jose

Linda

Julian

Sophie

Jade

Amber

Luisito

Julian

Beata

Atticus

Lorena

family tree

My parents Margot & Nestor

Luis Miguel

Me & my siblings

Cio

Grandma Mary & grandchildren

Cousin Miren

The Trápaga tribe

Grandma Mary

The Trápaga / Esteban clan in the 1970s

Ignatius

Margot

Oliver & Lola

Our wedding in New York

Lil & pig

Lil & Mon Chew

Me in Siena

Me & Atticus

Simon, Atticus & Oliver

Phoebe

Atticus & Mrs Beaver

Georgia, Victoria & Oliver

A well-stocked pantry is a beautiful thing. Like so many of their era, my parents always had a large walk-in pantry, and after enduring times of war and deprivation, it was a sense of comfort to them to have it filled with all the essentials. These days, with many people cooking less and so much pre-prepared food on offer, some of us no longer feel the need to have large supplies of staples on hand to turn into a meal. However, when you set up house for yourself, it makes good sense to keep a supply of basic non-perishable ingredients. Here is a list of what I keep, just to get you started:

Essentials:

- olive oil (I use a Spanish one)
- extra virgin olive oil
- sesame oil (for dressings and hummus)
- peanut oil or vegetable oil
- sherry vinegar, balsamic vinegar
- salt – both sea salt flakes and iodised salt
- black peppercorns (good to buy in bulk)
- soy sauce (both light and dark)
- a selection of dried pasta such as spaghetti, fusilli, farfalle, rigatoni, penne and fettuccine
- tomato paste
- canned tomatoes (buy these in bulk as you'll use them all the time)
- canned corn kernels and creamed corn
- canned tuna in oil
- canned beans, such as borlotti, cannellini, butter beans and chickpeas
- flour (both plain and self-raising)
- cornflour
- baking powder and bicarbonate of soda
- sugar (caster, brown, raw and icing)
- vanilla extract
- dried beans and pulses, such as lentils, lima beans, borlotti beans, mung beans, black-eyed beans, chickpeas, cannellini beans and haricot beans
- nuts, such as pine nuts, walnuts, peanuts and almonds

Non-essentials that you might find you need from time to time:

- dried fruit such as prunes, figs, dates and apricots
- walnut oil
- almond meal
- polenta
- desiccated coconut
- bread and butter pickles

For the liquor cabinet:

- Angostura bitters, sherry, port and brandy for cooking
- decent bottles of red and white wine for drinking
- I always keep a bottle each of gin, vodka, rum and Cointreau in the freezer and, in the fridge, lime cordial for cocktails and champagne for emergencies

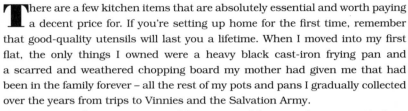

Cooking Utensils & Tips

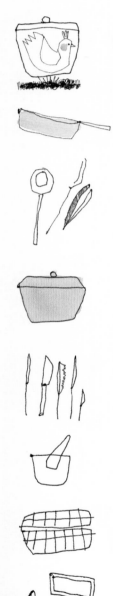

There are a few kitchen items that are absolutely essential and worth paying a decent price for. If you're setting up home for the first time, remember that good-quality utensils will last you a lifetime. When I moved into my first flat, the only things I owned were a heavy black cast-iron frying pan and a scarred and weathered chopping board my mother had given me that had been in the family forever – all the rest of my pots and pans I gradually collected over the years from trips to Vinnies and the Salvation Army.

A cast-iron frying pan is one of the most useful pieces of equipment to have in the kitchen. A well-seasoned pan will last you much longer so before you use it for the first time, wipe the inside with olive oil then heat it over a very high heat. Let the pan cool, wipe off any excess oil with a paper towel and repeat the process once more. Never wash the pan with detergent of any kind – just use hot water. A non-stick pan is also very useful for cooking eggs, pancakes and for stir-fries, but should be treated as if it were made of silk – no using with metal implements (wooden spoons and plastic egg flips are the way to go) and no cleaning with steel wool.

Another indispensable item in my kitchen is a good-quality flameproof casserole. My mother Margot has a classic orange Le Creuset that has been going strong for over 60 years – even surviving the ravages of the Second World War. Over the years I have amassed my own collection of these sturdy, beautiful pots that are perfect for slow-cooking, and I'll pass these down to my kids to use. If you treat them well, they will outlive you!

Don't be cheap when it comes to buying knives – good-quality knives are a sensible investment. Shop around and try before you buy, as they vary in weight and should feel comfortable in your hand. These days it is possible to find a knife block with a sharpener that will both store your knives and extend their life. Otherwise, try to buy a sharpener suited to your brand of knives, and always keep knives sharp – a blunt knife is far more dangerous than a sharp one.

My very favourite kitchen tool is an old-style coffee grinder that I've had for over twenty years. I use it everyday to grind peppercorns and spices – it has a little drawer to collect the ground spices, and you can adjust the size of the grind so it handles a variety of spices and seeds.

A good steamer will make life easy for you in the kitchen. The best ones have stackable steamer baskets so that you can steam different foods at the same time. Stainless-steel steamers are great but bamboo steamers are just as useful, cheaper and easily obtainable from Chinatown or Asian grocers.

When it comes to baking, I have three baking trays with shallow lips that are perfect for biscuits, meringues and slices. Remember that a sharp knife will score your trays so use caution when removing your freshly baked goodies.

Lining them with greaseproof paper will always give you a better result and extend the life of your trays.

I collect vintage eggbeaters and am rather partial to their magnificent design. They are generally easy to use and certainly keep the biceps toned – I for one am hoping to avoid 'tuckshop arms'! I also have a wonderful electric mixer that I use often, especially for meringues, butter creams and boiled icings.

A double boiler is perfect for melting chocolate or making custard, but you can use a heatproof bowl that fits over a saucepan of boiling water instead. When melting chocolate it is imperative that no moisture gets into the chocolate as it will make it 'blister' and change consistency, so take care that the bowl you use fits snugly over the pan and doesn't allow any moisture to escape.

The key to successful baking is to measure ingredients accurately. I recently moved into the twenty-first century and bought myself some battery-operated digital scales that measure grams, pounds and ounces. I learnt to cook in that in-between-time when measurements were changing over, and my scales have saved me many times when in need of a conversion. A set of standard measuring cups and a jug that has fluid ounces and cups marked on one side and millilitres on the other are also essential.

Last but not least is my fabulous little zester, a tool that can transform a dish with a flick of the wrist by adding a citrussy zing to sweet or savoury dishes. Zest can be used fresh for a glamorous garnish or it can be frozen for future use.

I use a lot of garlic in my cooking – and the fresher it is, the better. Sometimes it's hard to tell how fresh garlic is without cutting it in half. Many cloves of garlic have a green shoot in the middle which indicates that the garlic is old. It doesn't mean that the garlic is not still edible, but I always remove the green shoot as it is this that often gives people indigestion. I also generally chop my garlic over some salt to form a paste – this intensifies the flavour of the garlic. Although if I'm adding garlic to other salty ingredients, such as soy sauce, I will either crush it straight into the dish or substitute the salt for a little sugar. Always remember that garlic burns very easily so cook it over a low to medium heat.

I don't know any foodie worth their salt who doesn't keep a box of Maldon sea salt handy in the kitchen – I love the feeling of crushing the flakes between my fingers. However, there is an argument that plain old iodised salt has become so rare in many people's diets that there is an increasing rate of iodine deficiencies, so I keep both in easy reach on a shelf above the stove. The sea salt is superior and wonderful to flavour most dishes, but when I throw a great big pinch of salt into boiling water for pasta, I use the iodised salt as it's much more economical.

THE GUIDE LAW.

BE PREPARED

THE GUIDE PROMISE.

"ON MY HONOUR I promise that I will do my best—

1. To do my duty to God and the King.
2. To help other people at all times.
3. To obey the Guide Law."

BROWN, SON & FERGUSON, Ltd., Girl Guide Publishers
52-58 Darnley Street, GLASGOW

BROWN, SON & FERGUSON, Ltd., Girl Guide Publishers
52-58 Darnley Street, GLASGOW

AUGUST	1936				
Sun.	2	9	16	23	30
M.	3	10	17	24	31
T.	4	11	18	25	
W.	5	12	19	26	
T.	6	13	20	27	
F.	7	14	21	28	
S.	1	8	15	22	29

Sunrise and Sunset
Summer Time.
Aug. 1. Sun rises 5h. 25m. Sun sets 8h. 46m.
Aug. 15. Sun rises 5h. 47m. Sun sets 8h. 21m.

Moons
Full M. Aug. 3. Last Qtr. Aug. 9.
New M. Aug. 17. First Qtr. Aug. 25.

SEPTE	6	1			
Sun.	7	14	2		
M.	1	8	15	22	29
T.	2	9	16	23	30
W.	3	10	17	24	
T.	4	11	18	25	
F.	5	12	19	26	

Sunrise and Sunset
Summer Time.
Sept. 1. Sun rises 6h. 14m.
Sept. 1. Sun rises 7h. 45m.
Sept. 15. Sun rises 6h. 36m. Sun sets 7h. 14m.

Moons
Full M. Sept. 1. Last Qtr. Sept. 8.
New M. Sept. 15. First Qtr. Sept. 23.
Full M. Sept. 30.

THE MAN WHO WINS.

The man who wins is the average man,
Not built on any peculiar plan,
Not blest with any peculiar luck—
Just steady and earnest and full of
pluck.

When asked a question he does not
"guess"—
He knows the answers "No" or "Yes";
When set a task that the rest can't do,
He buckles down till he's put it
through.

Three things he's learned: that the
man who tries,
Finds favour in his employer's eyes;
That it pays to know more than one
thing well;
That it doesn't pay all he knows to tell.

So he works and waits, till one fine
day
There's a better job with bigger pay,
And the men who shirked whenever
they could
Are bossed by the man whose work
was good.

For the man who wins is the man who
works,
      labour   nor   trouble

Here's a selection of my favourite herbs to cook with. Try growing these in your garden or in pots and you'll always have fresh herbs to hand.

b a y

Laurus nobilis

Mistakenly believed to be a herb, bay leaves actually come from the sweet bay tree. Their strong, mysterious flavour enhances any marinade, stock, soup or casserole. I never boil potatoes without adding bay leaves, and always throw them into the pot when steaming rice.

b a s i l

c o r i a n d e r

Ocimum basilicum

Sweet basil is an annual grown easily from seed in warmer climates. If you only have space for a few herbs, be sure one of them is basil, as its flavour is incomparable, and I find it invaluable in the kitchen. Basil has a sweet, pungent aroma and a gentle, peppery taste. It's perfect in salads and with tomatoes, mozzarella, fish, chicken, mushrooms and, of course, made into pesto. Its flavour intensifies when cooked but used fresh, it will bring even the dullest ingredients to life. It is said that basil stimulates the appetite and aids digestion.

Coriandrum sativum

Coriander is a light-green feathery annual with lacy foliage. The leaves have a strong, sweet, distinct taste and the seeds are aromatic when crushed. Coriander leaves are commonly used in curries (they are said to aid digestion), and can be tossed through couscous or salads. I love to use ground coriander seeds, combined with other spices, to make a delicious marinade for fish, chicken, beef or pork.

c h i v e s

Allium schoenoprasum

A member of the onion family, chives grow in clumps from bulbs and have dark green, hollow, tube-like stems. They have a distinct onion flavour and are best used fresh; they make the perfect garnish for salads, scrambled eggs, sandwiches and canapés, and I use them chopped finely in sauces, dressings and mashed vegetables. Chives are said to reduce high blood pressure.

marjoram

Origanum majorana

From the same family as oregano, marjoram is an annual with small leaves that can be used either fresh or dried. It has a sweet, refreshing flavour and is my favourite herb to cook with. I love it with roast chicken, beef or pork or to flavour stews or braises. Fresh marjoram made into a tea is said to ease a sore throat.

mint

Mentha spicata

There are many varieties of mint, but spearmint, apple mint and peppermint are probably the most common. Mint is very prolific and should be contained in a pot as it will happily take over the whole garden. Its cool, menthol-like taste goes beautifully with lamb, peas, carrots, new potatoes and all kinds of fruit. Peppermint tea is well-known as a tonic for indigestion, and spearmint is said to improve the complexion and help eliminate skin disorders.

oregano

Origanum vulgare

Oregano is a low-growing, hardy herb with small, slightly furry leaves. In the kitchen, it works just as well in dried form as fresh. Its spicy warm peppery flavour is prized in Italian cooking as it marries so well with tomatoes, garlic and basil, and it is commonly used to flavour pizzas and pasta dishes. Oregano is said to stimulate the circulation.

parsley

Petroselinum crispum

Parsley is a biennial and there are two varieties commonly used in cooking: curly and flat-leaf. It has a refreshing, cleansing flavour, teams especially well with fish and is delicious in mayonnaise. Parsley is a rich source of vitamin C, protein, iron and minerals. It aids digestion and is said to ease arthritis and rheumatism. All this, and it gives you fresh breath too!

sage

Salvia officinalis

Sage is a very hardy perennial with large, silvery, slightly furry leaves growing on a medium-sized bush. With a cool, almost camphor-like flavour, it goes well with duck, lamb and pork and is wonderful in mashed potatoes and soups. It aids the digestion of fatty foods and is said to be good for colds and sore throats.

rosemary

Rosmarinus officinalis

An evergreen shrub with highly aromatic, needle-like leaves and woody stems, rosemary is best grown from a cutting or small plant as the seeds take a long time to germinate. I find its strong, pungent flavour wonderful with lamb, chicken, veal, beef, sausages and slow-roasted vegetables. Rosemary is said to be good for the skin and hair, and a tea made from it can help ease tension.

tarragon

Artemisia dracunculus

Tarragon has dark-green pointy leaves and grows into a medium-sized perennial shrub. It has a distinct aniseed flavour that the French adore (I prefer French tarragon to the coarse-leaved Russian tarragon, as it has a much more delicate flavour). It goes well with fish, chicken, steak, asparagus and artichokes, and is used in béarnaise and hollandaise sauce. It has often been said to be 'a friend to the head, heart and liver'.

thyme

Thymus vulgaris

Thyme is a low, spreading perennial bush with tiny mauve flowers. With an intense, antiseptic flavour, this herb is best used sparingly and enhances the flavour of sausages, soups, stews and stuffing wonderfully. Thyme is said to act as a diuretic and can aid the digestion of fatty foods.

SAUCES

BÉCHAMEL
Makes about 3 cups

The secret to a good béchamel lies in the roux – a paste made by stirring flour into melted butter over low heat, which forms the base of many French sauces, stews and soups.

Ingredients

4 cups milk
1 × 5 g onion and herb stock cube
  (I use Massel brand)
3 bay leaves
2 cloves garlic, finely chopped with
  1 teaspoon salt to make a paste
120 g butter
½ cup plain flour

Method

1 Combine the milk, stock cube, bay leaves and garlic paste in a saucepan and place over low heat to let the herbs steep in the milk for a few minutes.

2 Meanwhile, in a heavy-based saucepan, melt the butter then add the flour, stirring constantly over low heat – the paste (roux) will thicken and become sandy in texture. Remove from the heat and leave to cool.

3 Bring the milk mixture almost to a boil, then remove from the heat immediately and strain the liquid into a jug.

4 Put the roux back on the heat and gradually add the milk mixture, stirring between each addition to get rid of any lumps. I use a wooden spoon and give my biceps a good workout for this bit.

5 Keep stirring until all the milk has been added and the sauce has a thick, smooth consistency. Simmer, stirring, over very low heat for at least another 5 minutes.

MAYONNAISE
Makes 1½ cups

This is traditionally made with a mortar and pestle or in a bowl with a whisk to make it really light and fluffy, though I use a blender and it does the trick nicely. Herbs really give a lift to mayonnaise. Sometimes I add a tablespoon of pesto and it is really delicious. To make the French garlicky sauce aïoli, just throw in 2 cloves of crushed garlic with the egg yolks.

Ingredients

3 egg yolks (at room temperature)
1–1½ cups olive oil
juice of ½ a lemon
finely ground white pepper
1 tablespoon chopped tarragon or marjoram

Method

1 Place the the egg yolks in a blender, turn to the lowest setting and start to add the olive oil, firstly drop by drop and then in a steady stream. Keep adding oil until the mixture is thick and smooth.

2 While still blending on the lowest setting, add the lemon juice drop by drop, then season with finely ground white pepper. The mayonnaise is ready when the mixture resembles thick whipped cream.

3 If by chance the mixture curdles, put an extra egg yolk into a clean bowl, and slowly mix in the curdled sauce – you should get a nice, smooth result.

4 Stir in the herbs just before serving.

ALLIOLI

Makes 1½ cups

A true allioli is made with just garlic, olive oil and salt, but this can be devastating for one's social life, so really this is just a very garlicky mayonnaise. The lime juice gives it a very fresh, tart flavour that goes really well with seafood, but you could substitute lemon juice or wine vinegar instead, or add mustard or fresh herbs for a different flavour. My brother Ignatius often adds some chopped fresh tarragon to 3 tablespoons of white-wine vinegar, then reduces it in the micro-wave on high for 30 seconds and adds it drop by drop instead of the lime juice.

Ingredients

4 cloves garlic, finely chopped with
　½ teaspoon salt and ½ teaspoon sugar
　to make a paste
3 egg yolks (at room temperature)
1–1½ cups olive oil
juice of ½ a lime
finely ground white pepper

Method

1 Place the garlic paste and the egg yolks in a blender, turn to the lowest setting and start to add the olive oil, firstly drop by drop and then in a steady stream. Keep adding oil until the mixture is thick and smooth.

2 While still mixing on the lowest setting, add the lime juice drop by drop, then season with finely ground white pepper. The allioli is ready when the mixture resembles thick whipped cream.

3 If by chance the mixture curdles, put an extra egg yolk into a clean bowl, and slowly mix in the curdled sauce – you should get a nice, smooth result.

PESTO

Makes 1½ cups

Pesto is one of those recipes where all the ingredients combine to create the ultimate pasta sauce. It's also wonderful drizzled on roasted vegetables or mixed with some cream cheese for a scrumptious dip. The ingredients can vary – some people replace the basil with coriander or rosemary, and the pine nuts with walnuts or hazelnuts – but I think the classic version below is absolutely perfect as it is.

If serving pesto with pasta, I use an Italian dried fusilli or penne. I often make more than required as my children always want it for lunch the following day, and it's one dish that is good served hot or cold.

Ingredients

85 g pine nuts
1 large bunch fresh basil, leaves picked,
　well washed
3 cloves garlic, crushed
1 cup grated parmesan cheese
¾ cup olive oil
sea salt and freshly ground black pepper
juice of ½ a lemon

Method

1 Roast the pine nuts by placing them on a plate in the microwave. Cook on the highest setting for 1 minute, then check them – they should just be starting to colour. Cook on the highest setting for a further minute, or until they turn golden, then set aside to cool.

2 Pat the basil leaves dry with paper towel. Place them in a blender, add the rest of the ingredients and purée to a thick paste.

When we were kids, pancakes punctuated our Sundays. After attending the 6 p.m. mass we would come home and Mum would start making the batter while my brothers fought over the frying pan. They would compete to see who could flip the highest pancake. Inevitably, some ended up on the floor and were given to our bull-terrier, Brunhilde. I hated church but I loved Sundays. They were always noisy and slightly chaotic but a lot of fun. Whenever I smell maple syrup, wonderful memories of those sticky Sundays come rushing back.

Now I often make pancakes for my clan, and I'm constantly experimenting with the recipe. Sometimes I use fresh ricotta, and sometimes I replace the regular milk with buttermilk. This recipe is pretty foolproof, but the secret is to combine the juice of a lemon with the milk – this curdles it and makes the pancakes lighter. If, when you flip your pancake, the underside is blackened, you'll know the heat is too high. Turn it down, wipe your pan out with a paper towel and a little butter, and start again.

Ingredients

2 cups self-raising flour
pinch salt
2 tablespoons
   caster sugar
2 large eggs, separated
2 cups milk
juice of 1 lemon
40 g butter, melted,
   plus extra for cooking
1 teaspoon
   vanilla extract
lemon wedges and sugar
   or pure maple syrup
   and roughly chopped
   toasted pecan nuts,
   to serve

Method

1 Sift the flour and salt into a medium-sized mixing bowl. Sprinkle the sugar over the top and create a well in the centre. Place the egg yolks in the well. Mix the milk and lemon juice together in a jug and stir with a fork; the mixture should curdle a little. Pour a splash of the milk mixture in the centre of the flour well and combine the ingredients with a wooden spoon. Repeat until all the milk mixture is used – you should end up with a smooth batter.

2 Beat the eggwhites in a large bowl until stiff peaks form, then fold into the batter along with the melted butter and the vanilla. Transfer the batter to a jug and chill in the fridge for half an hour.

3 To cook the pancakes, heat a small amount of butter in a non-stick frying pan (just enough to coat the pan). Pour some batter into the pan (the amount will depend on how big you want your pancakes, remembering the bigger the pancake, the harder it is to flip – I find that about a 15 cm diameter is manageable). Wait for bubbles to form on top, and as soon as they burst, flip the pancake. Let it cook for about a minute more, or until golden on the underside, then remove and place on a warmed plate. Cover with a clean tea towel while you cook the rest, then serve with lemon and sugar or maple syrup and pecan nuts.

Makes about 12

During my late twenties, I spent the majority of my time touring Australia performing concerts for children. Although appearing in a different town every day was exhausting, one of the great perks was the constant culinary kindness I experienced. In those little country towns, perfectly baked scones and mouth-watering slices would be offered for morning tea. Homemade jams were served on bread still hot from the oven. Home-grown quinces, preserved and teamed with rich vanilla custard (a deep yellow colour from the free-range eggs), and freshly picked cherries were kindly packed into our van along with sad farewells.

I prefer the country to the big smoke any day. When touring cities, the only comfort that I really love in fancy city hotels is Bircher muesli – I just can't help myself, I have to try it. So now that I'm not away so much, I make my own Bircher muesli. Throw this together in the evening and chill overnight for a really intense-flavoured breakfast the next morning.

Method

1 Put the grated apple in a ceramic mixing bowl and pour over the orange juice and honey to stop the apple browning, then refrigerate.

2 In a separate bowl, combine the rest of the ingredients except the cinnamon and strawberries and chill in the fridge for an hour or two.

3 Mix the oat and apple mixtures together, add a sprinkle of cinnamon, then cover with plastic film and chill overnight.

4 Just before serving, give the muesli a good stir then serve as is or garnish with some thinly sliced strawberries. This is a generous recipe and this batch should last a few days (the great thing is that it tastes even better each day as the flavours mingle).

Serves 6

Ingredients

4 granny smith apples, peeled and grated

1 cup freshly squeezed orange juice

2 tablespoons honey

500 g rolled oats (try to get organic oats)

½ cup pitted prunes

½ cup dried apricots

½ cup sultanas or dried cranberries

½ cup ground hazelnuts

1 cup slivered almonds

2 cups good-quality vanilla yoghurt

cinnamon, to sprinkle

thinly sliced strawberries (optional), to garnish

S.A.N.D.W.I.C.H.E.S

Life is too short for boring sammies, so here are
some of my favourite combinations. My local bakery
and cafe, Sonoma, makes the best spelt bread from
naturally leavened sourdough that is perfect teamed
with really fresh ingredients. Try and get some from
your local bakery if you can.

Smoked ham or turkey,
brie, spring onion,
cranberry sauce and
pistachios

Jamón, manchego cheese
and baby spinach

Smoked chicken,
mayonnaise, rocket
and spring onion

Bacon, avocado,
butter lettuce
and freshly ground
black pepper

Turkey, beetroot relish,
camembert and pickles

Tuna, mayonnaise
and lettuce

Smoked salmon,
cream cheese,
chives and capers

Peanut butter,
bananas, honey
and sultanas

Jamón or pastrami,
strong cheddar cheese
and baby spinach

ZUCCHINI & CORN FRITTERS

Makes 15 fritters!

When my daughter Lil was 21, in her last year of uni and itching to have her own place, I offered her my house in Arcadia Road, Glebe, to rent with four of her friends, as I had just moved in with Simon. With good intentions and little experience, they set up a very kooky home.

The pantry in a share-house will always yield an interesting collection of food. In Arcadia Road it was a lifetime's supply of tinned tomatoes and enough kidney beans to put a hole in the ozone layer. One of Lil's housemates, Vesna, would bring home boxes of organic vegetables, some of which they couldn't even identify, let alone cook. Peta and Hannah were the vegetarians of the house, always finding new and exotic ways to cook kidney beans. And when Alex moved in, Lil was so excited to find a flatmate with similar tastebuds – they both hankered for garlic bread, trying every style available at the supermarket. Then there was Loki, their honorary housemate, who would stay every Tuesday night, clearing out the fridge in true locust fashion, making sure no leftovers were overlooked. I have never seen last week's sausages disappear so quickly.

One genuine winner was Peta's zucchini and corn fritters. They normally never reached the table as the girls would munch on them as soon as they came out of the pan. Peta took to cooking double batches that would satisfy their starved student stomachs and provide lunchbox treats for the next day. If you like fluffy fritters, use self-raising flour, but if you like them flatter and denser, use plain flour. You can top these fritters with anything from avocado and fresh basil leaves to sour cream, tomato relish or hummus.

Ingredients

1 cob fresh sweetcorn or
  1 × 250 g can corn, drained
3 zucchinis, grated
20 g melted butter
1–1½ cups plain or
  self-raising flour
1 egg
½ cup milk, plus extra if needed
½ teaspoon ground cumin
sea salt and freshly ground black pepper
oil, for frying

Method

1 If using fresh sweetcorn, stand the cob on its end and carefully cut off the kernels with a knife.

2 Place the corn kernels in a microwave-safe bowl with a little water and cook for 3 minutes on high, then drain.

3 Squeeze out any extra moisture from the grated zucchini and mix with the cooked or canned corn in a bowl, then stir in the melted butter.

4 Add the flour a quarter of a cup at a time, mixing to coat the vegetables thoroughly (you may not need to use it all – stop adding when the mixture no longer absorbs the flour). Crack the egg into the bowl and combine, then pour in the milk and combine – the mixture should be runny enough to pour off a spoon. Add the cumin and salt and pepper to taste, then mix well.

5 Heat a thin layer of oil in a large frying pan. Drop in dessertspoonfuls of batter and spread out to form palm-sized rounds. Cook fritters on both sides until golden brown.

6 Taste-test the first round of fritters to see if more cumin, salt or pepper is required – if so, stir some more into the batter before you cook the rest.

PUMPKIN & GINGER SOUP

I get so many compliments on this soup that I just had to include it. It's light yet very satisfying, and puréed in the blender it becomes very creamy without the addition of any dairy products. This soup can be made in advance and frozen, and it also works as a delicious chilled soup in summer.

Method

1 In a large pan with a lid, heat the butter and olive oil over medium heat, then fry the leeks, covered, for 5 minutes. Reduce the heat to low and continue to cook until softened.

2 Add the garlic and ginger pastes and fry briefly, stirring to make sure they don't burn. Toss the pumpkin in the pan and mix well. Add 6 cups water and bring the soup to a boil, then reduce the heat to a rolling simmer and cook for 1 hour, stirring occasionally.

3 Add the pepper and taste for seasoning. Turn off the heat and let the soup cool for about 30 minutes, then purée in batches in a blender until smooth. If you like a chunkier soup, mash it by hand with a potato masher.

4 Gently reheat then serve with a sprinkle of chopped chives or coriander and a grinding of pepper.

Serves 6

Ingredients

- 40 g butter
- 2 tablespoons olive oil
- 2 leeks, trimmed and well washed, white part finely sliced
- 3 cloves garlic, finely chopped with ½ teaspoon salt and ½ teaspoon sugar to make a paste
- 2 × 4 cm knobs ginger, finely chopped with ½ teaspoon salt and ½ teaspoon sugar to make a paste
- 1.7 kg pumpkin, peeled and chopped into small cubes
- 1 teaspoon freshly ground black pepper, plus extra
- chopped chives or coriander, to serve

Sweet Potato, Rocket & Goat's Curd Salad

Sweet potato would have to be one of the most satisfying and versatile vegetables around. There is so much to be made of this humble, orange-fleshed tuber. Mashed with a bit of cream and butter and a pinch of nutmeg, made into chips or served in a salad – it's always sensational.

This salad is simple to make and goes well with any kind of roast meat. I love it as a meal on its own or as a first course. The goat's curd can be replaced with a goat's milk feta which is less expensive and has an equally good flavour.

Ingredients

3 cups baby rocket, washed
2 large sweet potatoes, diced and slow-roasted (see page 96), cooled to room temperature
150 g goat's curd or goat's-milk feta
¾ cup roasted walnuts (optional)

Dressing

6 cloves slow-roasted garlic (see page 96)
¼ cup extra virgin olive oil
¼ cup balsamic vinegar
½ teaspoon caster sugar
juice of ½ a lemon
sea salt and freshly ground black pepper

Method

1 To make the dressing, squeeze the soft insides from the roasted garlic into a bowl and discard the skin. Add the rest of the ingredients and whisk with a fork until well combined.

2 Place the rocket in a large salad bowl and toss through the sweet potato. Crumble the goat's curd or feta and the walnuts, if using, over the top.

3 Pour half the dressing over the salad and toss through. If this seems like enough, then it's ready to serve, however if it looks a little dry pour the remaining dressing on, give it another toss and serve. You can save any leftover dressing in the fridge to use another time – it should keep for about a week. Just bring it to room temperature before adding to the salad.

Serves 4–6

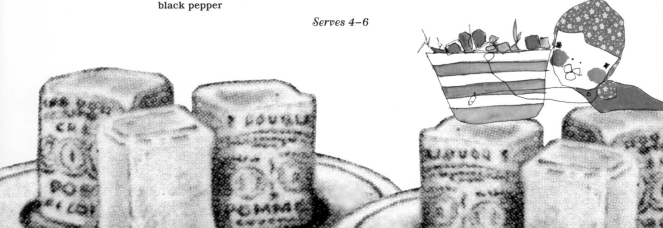

This is one of those delicious, healthy meals that is cheap and easy to throw together but can make you feel like a million dollars. The recipe comes from a great family friend, Nicki, who has always been an inspiration to me when it comes to food and celebration – the first time I went to one of her parties she'd made an entire bathtubful of trifle for dessert!

Nicki was always entertaining the hordes in her beautiful house, and as a consequence Lil spent many of her childhood years running around the back garden with Nicki's kids – building hideouts, catching rabbits, learning to backward somersault into the pool. We've shared many special meals with Nicki and her family over the years but funnily enough this simple salad is one of the most memorable, with its delicious vibrant flavours.

The secret here is to get tuna canned in oil, which you drain off and mix with fresh lime and, hey presto, the dressing is done. When I made this recently I grated a big knob of fresh ginger over the top before adding the lime juice – it was really refreshing and perfect for a summer's night.

Method

1 Top and tail the green beans and steam for a few minutes, then plunge into iced water. Place the rest of the ingredients, except the lime juice and the tuna oil, in a salad bowl.

2 Mix the lime juice and tuna oil together and pour over the salad. Season and toss the salad well so the dressing coats all the ingredients. Serve immediately.

Serves 4

Ingredients

handful green beans

1 iceberg lettuce, chopped into bite-sized pieces

1 × 400 g can tuna in oil, drained, oil reserved

3 just-ripe avocados, peeled and chopped

4 sticks celery, chopped

2 carrots, cut into thin strips

4 roma tomatoes, cut into quarters

2 red capsicums, white insides and seeds removed, diced

½ cup pitted black olives

juice of 2 limes

sea salt and freshly ground black pepper

Spectacular Spaghetti Bolognese

There has always been a bit of competition in our family as to who makes the best bolognese, and with a family as big as ours there have been many variations! I am convinced that the secret is to use three different types of meat, and to let them slowly caramelise as you cook them. The longer you cook the sauce the better, as the flavours will intensify. This recipe will feed at least six, with a little leftover for tomorrow's lunch.

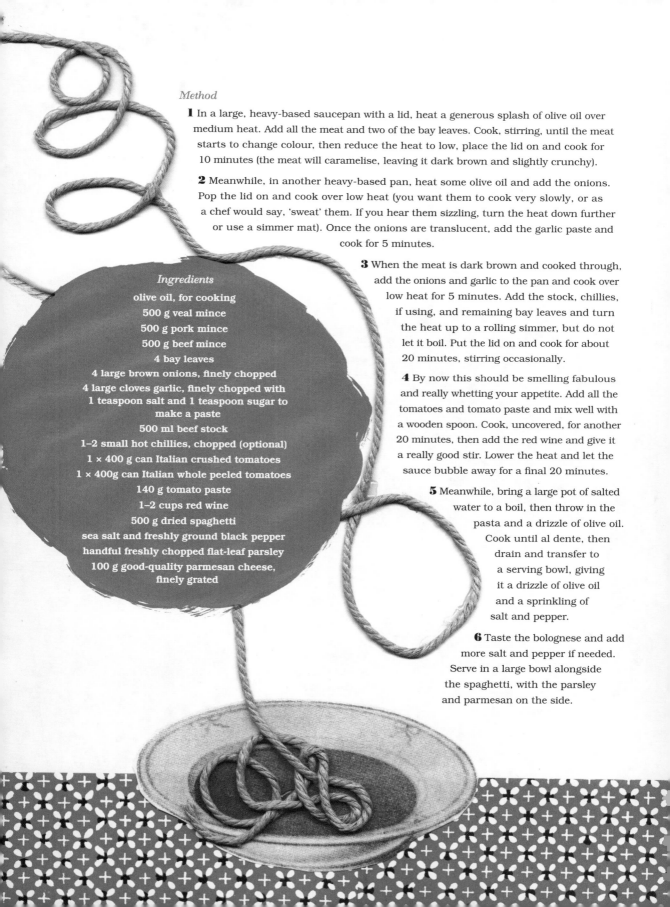

Method

1 In a large, heavy-based saucepan with a lid, heat a generous splash of olive oil over medium heat. Add all the meat and two of the bay leaves. Cook, stirring, until the meat starts to change colour, then reduce the heat to low, place the lid on and cook for 10 minutes (the meat will caramelise, leaving it dark brown and slightly crunchy).

2 Meanwhile, in another heavy-based pan, heat some olive oil and add the onions. Pop the lid on and cook over low heat (you want them to cook very slowly, or as a chef would say, 'sweat' them. If you hear them sizzling, turn the heat down further or use a simmer mat). Once the onions are translucent, add the garlic paste and cook for 5 minutes.

3 When the meat is dark brown and cooked through, add the onions and garlic to the pan and cook over low heat for 5 minutes. Add the stock, chillies, if using, and remaining bay leaves and turn the heat up to a rolling simmer, but do not let it boil. Put the lid on and cook for about 20 minutes, stirring occasionally.

4 By now this should be smelling fabulous and really whetting your appetite. Add all the tomatoes and tomato paste and mix well with a wooden spoon. Cook, uncovered, for another 20 minutes, then add the red wine and give it a really good stir. Lower the heat and let the sauce bubble away for a final 20 minutes.

5 Meanwhile, bring a large pot of salted water to a boil, then throw in the pasta and a drizzle of olive oil. Cook until al dente, then drain and transfer to a serving bowl, giving it a drizzle of olive oil and a sprinkling of salt and pepper.

6 Taste the bolognese and add more salt and pepper if needed. Serve in a large bowl alongside the spaghetti, with the parsley and parmesan on the side.

Ingredients

olive oil, for cooking
500 g veal mince
500 g pork mince
500 g beef mince
4 bay leaves
4 large brown onions, finely chopped
4 large cloves garlic, finely chopped with 1 teaspoon salt and 1 teaspoon sugar to make a paste
500 ml beef stock
1–2 small hot chillies, chopped (optional)
1 × 400 g can Italian crushed tomatoes
1 × 400g can Italian whole peeled tomatoes
140 g tomato paste
1–2 cups red wine
500 g dried spaghetti
sea salt and freshly ground black pepper
handful freshly chopped flat-leaf parsley
100 g good-quality parmesan cheese, finely grated

Red Capsicum & Sherry Chicken with Rice

My mother Margot juggled four children, a full-time teaching job, a part-time university degree and a Spanish husband – I now understand why this quick and simple Spanish dish was one of her favourites. A fresh chilli thrown in with the capsicum will add a little Asian zing. Prepare this in the morning before you leave for work so it can marinate all day.

Method

1 In a large shallow dish, mix the cornflour with the sherry, salt and pepper. Add the chicken, cover and marinade in the fridge for at least 8 hours.

2 Put the rice in a saucepan with a lid and cover with cold water. Swish the rice around in the water to rinse, and then slowly pour the water out (being careful not to lose any rice down the sink). Place your middle fingertip directly on the surface of the rice and fill with water up to your finger's first joint. Bring to a boil, then turn the heat down to the lowest setting, cover and cook for 10–12 minutes. Leave covered until ready to serve.

3 In a heavy-based frying pan or wok, heat a little olive oil over medium heat. Toss in the capsicum and fry for 1 minute, then remove with a slotted spoon and set aside.

4 Add a little more oil to the pan and turn the heat up to high. Add the chicken, reserving the marinade, and toss for a couple of minutes until just cooked. Return the capsicum to the pan and add a splash of the marinade, stirring until all the ingredients are combined. Heat through for a minute or two, then serve immediately on a bed of rice with steamed green beans or asparagus on the side.

Serves 6

Ingredients

¼ cup cornflour

2 cups medium–sweet sherry

1 teaspoon sea salt

1 teaspoon freshly ground black pepper

3 large chicken breasts, skin removed, cut into small cubes (try to get organic if you can)

3 cups long-grain rice

olive oil, for cooking

2 red capsicums, white insides and seeds removed, diced

steamed green beans or asparagus, to serve

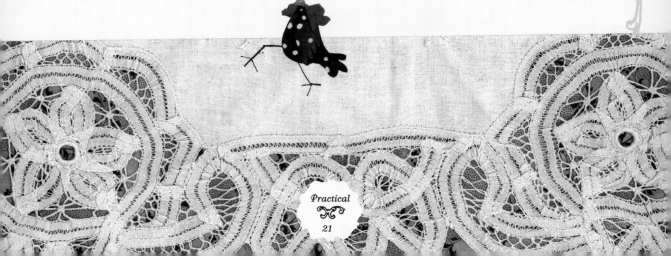

A Word on Beef

Cooking a beef roast is an art form that can only be mastered with plenty of practice. Beef is expensive and therefore should be treated with care and patience in order to get the best out of it. When I am at the butcher's I ask lots of questions about the beef I'm buying – the simplest tip can be the difference between an average roast and a sensational feast. (And I have never met a butcher I didn't like, as charm and a flirtatious nature seem to be part of their job description!)

The important questions to ask about beef are:

* Is it grain-fed or grass-fed? (Grass-fed beef has loads more flavour and is usually chemical-free.)
* How old is it? Is it yearling, prime or mature beef? (This will have an impact on the way you cook it.)
* How much of it will I need to feed the family?

This diagram shows you which part of the cow each cut of meat comes from:

chuck, blade · fore rib · flank · sirloin · rump · silverside · thick flank · topside · neck · thick rib · shin · oxtail

Knowing which part of the cow your cut of beef comes from will arm you with the knowledge of how long you need to cook it and whether or not you should sear it before roasting. The golden rule to remember here is that fat (marbling) equals flavour. A cut of meat from a part of the animal that gets plenty of exercise will contain more muscle than fat and generally have less flavour, whereas a cut from an area that is not exercised much will have a greater amount of fat. That is why wagyu beef is so expensive – it has a very high degree of marbling. (In fact, owing to limited space on Japanese farms, they say the farmers used to massage the cattle to avoid leg cramps, and add beer and saki to the food to increase the cattle's appetites in humid weather. Lucky beasts! But I digress...)

A sirloin fillet is the most tender cut of beef but I find it has less flavour than a cut on the bone. If I'm going to roast a beef fillet I splash out and buy a scotch fillet (or rib eye, from the fore rib), which tends to have more flavour than the sirloin. The secret is to start with the meat at room temperature and to sear it in olive oil in a heavy-based pan over high heat (this seals in the juices and increases the overall flavour). Transfer to a 200°C oven until cooked to your liking, then leave the meat to rest, covered in foil, for at least 30 minutes. I've always said that a beef fillet is easy to cook but even easier to overcook – it needs a lot less cooking than a roast on the bone, and should be cooked to medium–rare at most.

For a roast to feed the hordes, an economical cut to use is yearling topside. It usually comes as a big chunky triangle of beef that will produce a decent amount of meat. It's perfect for roasting and the leftovers are good in sandwiches.

For a really special occasion, it's worth splashing out on a fabulous cut like a standing rib roast from the forequarter or a wing-ribbed sirloin from the hindquarter. I always ask my butcher how long to cook these for as it varies depending on the quality of the meat and the size of the cut.

Beef Roast with Red Wine & Slow-roasted Fennel or Leeks

I usually make this with fennel, but as my husband Simon doesn't eat it I recently tried substituting leeks instead and the result was delicious. Try it either way – both are scrumptious. You'll need to start preparing this the morning of the day you want to eat it as the meat has to stand for a few hours before cooking.

Ingredients

2 cups red wine

8 cloves garlic

2 sprigs thyme

1 kg beef scotch fillet, tied with string (ask your butcher to do this for you)

2 sprigs rosemary

olive oil, for cooking

sea salt and freshly ground black pepper

3 bay leaves

2 large fennel bulbs, trimmed and sliced diagonally into 2 cm pieces *or* 2–3 leeks, trimmed, well washed and sliced into 3 cm pieces

50 g butter

1 tablespoon plain flour

steamed asparagus, to serve

Method

1 On the morning of the day you want to serve this, take a small baking tray with a rack and pour the red wine into the bottom of the tray. Peel 4 cloves of garlic, removing any green sprout from the middle, and slice each clove into three chunks. Push the garlic chunks, along with the leaves from one sprig of thyme, into the folds of the meat. Place the rosemary sprigs on the rack and sit the meat on top. Rub the outside of the fillet all over with olive oil and sprinkle on some pepper. Tuck the bay leaves and remaining thyme sprigs under the string on top of the fillet, then cover the fillet and the baking tray with foil and refrigerate for at least 6 hours.

2 Preheat the oven to 150°C. Take the baking tray from the fridge, remove and discard the bay leaves and thyme sprigs and leave the meat to come to room temperature.

3 Arrange the fennel or leek in a large buttered baking dish, dot with 30 g butter and add the remaining 4 cloves of garlic. Season with salt and pepper and cover with a lid or foil and bake for 45 minutes.

4 Remove the fennel or leek from the oven and set aside, still covered. Increase the oven temperature to 200°C. In a heavy-based frying pan, heat olive oil over high heat until very hot. Sear the fillet for a few seconds on all sides until golden brown (reserving the wine and meat juices in the baking tray to make the gravy later). Pick the leaves from the sprig of rosemary and set aside.

5 Uncover the fennel or leek and spoon out any liquid that has gathered in the dish and reserve. Place the seared fillet on the fennel or leek in the baking dish, then drizzle the reserved vegetable liquid over the top. Season with salt, sprinkle with the rosemary leaves and roast for 15 minutes. Remove the fillet from the dish and set it aside, covered with foil, on a large plate.

6 Cook the fennel or leek for a further 20 minutes, then remove from the oven and set aside, once again draining off and reserving the cooking juices. Heat the remaining butter and the flour in a frying pan over medium heat, stirring with a wooden spoon to make a paste (called a roux). Gradually add the reserved cooking liquid from the fennel or leek to the roux, stirring to remove any lumps. Add a cup of the reserved wine and meat juices as well as any juices from the resting meat. Bring to a boil and simmer for about 5–10 minutes until the gravy has thickened and reduced. Taste for seasoning then pour into a jug to serve.

7 Remove any chunks of garlic from the fillet and carve the meat into ½ cm thick slices. Serve with a generous spoonful of fennel or leek, some steamed asparagus and a drizzle of gravy.

Serves 4–6

Julian's French Green Beans

I have always loved my ex-husband Julian's cooking; he really works hard to perfect his favourite dishes. One of his specialties was French green beans. These are wonderful with a roast chicken or coq au vin, and are especially good with a slow-cooked sticky lamb dish like the one opposite, as they add a lovely freshness.

I have also made this dish with the same amount of slivered almonds in place of the breadcrumbs and it worked beautifully.

Ingredients

800 g fresh finest-quality French green beans, topped and tailed

⅓ cup extra virgin olive oil

3 cloves garlic, crushed

⅓ cup breadcrumbs

¼–⅓ cup finely chopped flat-leaf parsley

sea salt and freshly ground black pepper

60 g butter

Method

1 Drop the beans in a large pan of salted boiling water and cook them for about 6 minutes, or until al dente. While they are cooking, fill another large pan with iced water.

2 Drain the beans in a colander then immerse the colander into the pan of iced water. This will stop the beans from cooking and help them keep their vibrant green colour.

3 In a large, heavy-based frying pan or wok, heat the olive oil over low heat and fry the garlic, breadcrumbs and parsley with a pinch of salt and pepper. Cook, stirring, until the garlic starts to turn golden. Add the butter and as soon as it melts, stir in the beans. Toss the beans until they are heated through and evenly coated with the breadcrumb mixture, then serve immediately.

Serves 6 as a side dish

Slow-cooked Sticky Lamb Shanks with Parsnips

round April, when the weather turns and autumn is upon us, the light in my kitchen suddenly seems different, and the chill in the air inspires me to cook lamb. I love lamb shanks, and the longer you cook them, the better. I have a fire-engine-red Le Creuset casserole with a matching lid that never ceases to catch the eye of anybody entering the kitchen. Just about anything I cook in this casserole is a triumph, especially meat and poultry – the flavours are always particularly intense. Cooking this dish seems to warm the whole household, and when you take the lid off, the fragrance is explosive.

If you are serving more than four people, allow one shank per person and increase the veggies to your liking. I like to serve this with a big spoonful of brown rice to soak up the delicious sauce.

Method

1 Preheat the oven to 180°C.

2 Pour a generous drizzle of olive oil into a large, ovenproof heavy-based saucepan or a flame-proof casserole and mix in the salt, pepper, powdered vegetable stock and garlic. Add the lamb shanks and massage the oil mixture into the meat. Add the vegetables, bay leaves and rosemary, pour in the wine and mix gently until all ingredients are combined. Cover with a lid and cook in the oven for 1 hour.

3 Carefully remove the casserole from the oven, lift the lid and gently turn the shanks and the veggies so everything gets a chance to cook evenly. Pour in 1 cup water, cover and return the casserole to the oven for another hour.

4 Turn the shanks and veggies again, add another cup of water and cook for a further hour before serving.

Serves 4

Ingredients

olive oil, for cooking

sea salt and freshly ground
  black pepper

1 tablespoon powdered
  vegetable stock

6 cloves garlic, peeled
  and cut in half

4 lamb shanks

2 sticks celery, cut into
  6 cm pieces

3 leeks, trimmed and well
  washed, white parts sliced
  into 3 cm pieces

3 parsnips, cut in half
  lengthways then sliced
  into 5 cm pieces

3 large carrots, cut in half
  lengthways then sliced
  into 5 cm pieces

6 golden shallots,
  cut in half lengthways

6 bay leaves

2 sprigs rosemary

3 glasses Riesling or other
  dry white wine

MRS B'S PISTACHIO & CHOCOLATE CAKE

There are certain foods that individually are wonderful but, when combined, are truly spectacular. This cake is one of those special combinations. My former nanny/tour manager/PA, Mrs Beaver, used to make this for me on my birthday. If you ever come across a pear liqueur (such as poire William), squirrel it away and serve it with this cake to someone special, and I can guarantee good things will happen.

This cake hardly needs icing, but if you want it to be extra special, melt 250 g dark chocolate with 200 ml thickened cream over a double boiler (or a bowl that fits snugly over a saucepan of boiling water) and stir until smooth and glossy. Otherwise, cream whipped with a teaspoon of vanilla extract, 2 tablespoons of caster sugar and a generous sprinkling of pistachio praline would be equally impressive.

Ingredients

1¼ cups plain flour
1 teaspoon baking powder
¾ cup caster sugar
pinch salt
150 g unsalted butter
3 eggs
200 g dark chocolate,
  broken into small pieces
1 pear, peeled, cored
  and diced
¾ cup pistachio nuts
finely grated zest
  of 1 orange

Method

1 Preheat oven to 180°C and butter and flour a 22 cm × 11.5 cm loaf tin.

2 Put the flour, baking powder, sugar, salt, butter and eggs in a food processor and mix until just combined. Transfer the mixture to a bowl and fold in the chocolate, pear, pistachios and orange zest until combined.

3 Pour the batter into the prepared tin and bake for 50–60 minutes until a skewer inserted in the centre comes out clean. Leave the cake in the tin to cool then turn out onto a wire rack.

Serves 8

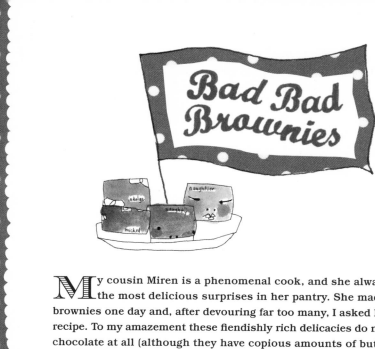

Bad Bad Brownies

My cousin Miren is a phenomenal cook, and she always has the most delicious surprises in her pantry. She made these brownies one day and, after devouring far too many, I asked her for the recipe. To my amazement these fiendishly rich delicacies do not contain chocolate at all (although they have copious amounts of butter), and are pretty much created in one pan. If you wanted to really make them sinful you could throw in a handful of chocolate chips just before you put them in the oven, but after much discussion we both agreed that they are perfect just as they are.

These wicked little devils make a great afternoon-tea treat or a decadent midnight feast with a very cold glass of milk.

Method

1 Preheat the oven to 180°C and line a 20 cm × 30 cm baking tray with greaseproof paper.

2 Melt the butter with the cocoa over a low heat, mixing with a wooden spoon until smooth, then remove from the heat and set aside.

3 Beat the eggs well, then add the sugar and beat a little more. Add the sifted flour and vanilla to the egg mixture and combine until smooth. Fold in the melted butter and cocoa and the nuts, if using. Pour mixture into the lined baking tray and cook for about 35 minutes, or until just springy to the touch.

4 Remove from the oven and leave to cool for 20 minutes in the tray before dusting with icing sugar and cutting into squares. Turn out once cooled completely.

Makes 24

Ingredients

350 g butter

140 g unsweetened cocoa

6 eggs

675 g caster sugar

250 g plain flour, sifted

3 teaspoons vanilla extract

100 g walnuts (optional)

icing sugar, for dusting

SHORTBREAD

My mother taught me to make these when I was ten years old. It is the simplest recipe I know and can be made in the blink of an eye.

Ingredients

250 g butter
1 cup sugar
2 cups plain flour
1 tablespoon vanilla extract
finely grated zest of 1 lemon
milk, for brushing

Method

1 Preheat the oven to 180°C.
2 Cream the butter and sugar together until light and fluffy. Add the flour, vanilla and lemon zest and mix to form a smooth dough.
3 Press the dough into a biscuit tray and bake for 12–15 minutes or until golden brown.
4 Remove from the oven and lightly brush the top with milk. Cut into diamond shapes, then leave to cool before turning out.

Makes 24

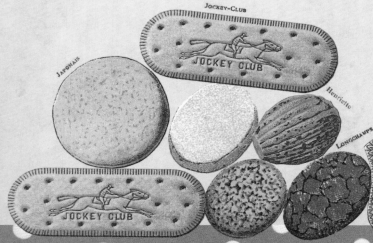

Practical

WALNUT COOKIES

Out of
all the nuts, I love
walnuts the most and find
that they lend a dark, mysterious
flavour to sweet recipes. As they are often
teamed with ingredients such as brown sugar,
cinnamon, coffee, apples or dates, it seems
they are rarely allowed to stand alone and be
appreciated for their unique flavour. So this recipe,
given to me by my sister Cio, celebrates the walnut.
The recipe calls for walnut oil, which is not
cheap and can be hard to find (try health food
stores or specialist food suppliers). Although
a bit of an investment, the oil adds something
really special to these biscuits, and is also
sensational in salad dressings and
a great substitute for some of the
olive oil in pesto sauce.

Ingredients

125 g butter, softened
⅔ cup caster sugar
100 ml walnut oil
½ teaspoon vanilla extract
¼ teaspoon salt
1 egg
250 g self-raising flour
90 g ground walnuts
icing sugar, for dusting

Method

1 Cream the butter,
sugar and walnut oil together
until light and fluffy. Add the vanilla,
salt and egg and mix thoroughly. Sift in the
flour, add the nuts and combine.
2 Roll the dough into a log-shape on a piece of
greaseproof paper and wrap the paper around it, then
wrap in plastic film and freeze for 30 minutes.
3 Preheat the oven to 180°C and
butter two 28 cm × 43 cm biscuit trays.
4 Unwrap the dough, cut into 3 mm-thick slices and
place on the biscuit trays. Bake for 8–10 minutes
or until golden brown. Dust with icing sugar
and serve with a strong coffee.

Makes 24

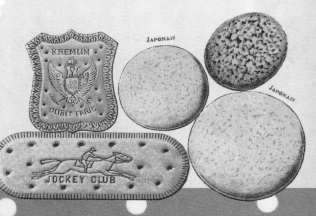

KREMLIN
OLIBET PARIS

JAPONAIS

JAPONAIS

Henriette

LILLOIS

JOCKEY CLUB

One of the reasons I always make a fuss of birthdays is because mine falls on the 30th of December – a lousy time of year to be born. Invariably, most people forget my birthday amidst the chaos of the festive season, and if I want to have a party or celebration I have to organise it months ahead to be sure everyone can be there.

For all my talk about my disastrous birthdays, Lil has a Teledex-like memory that has them filed away in chronological order. For one birthday she had painstakingly baked me a lemon slice and used double the butter by mistake – resulting in a rather greasy, stodgy affair. I was so touched that she had gone to so much effort that I ate a very large portion with sincere enthusiasm, but couldn't face lemon slice for years to come.

So this is that recipe, adapted from one I saw years ago in a book all about lemons by American chef Christopher Idone – very rich but with the right amount of butter this time.

Ingredients

Shortbread Base
3½ cups plain flour
¼ teaspoon salt
¼ cup icing sugar
350 g butter

Filling
6 large eggs
2 cups caster sugar
1 tablespoon finely
  grated lemon zest
½ cup lemon juice
⅔ cup plain flour
1 teaspoon baking powder
icing sugar, for dusting

Method

1 Preheat the oven to 200˚C.

2 For the shortbread base, sift the flour, salt and icing sugar into a large bowl. Cut the butter into chunks and gradually add to the flour mixture, mixing in with a pastry blender or rubbing together with your fingers.

3 Press the dough into a baking tin that is at least 3 cm deep (you don't have to grease the pan as this recipe already contains a lot of butter). Bake for about 12–15 minutes until golden, then remove from the oven, but leave the oven on.

4 Meanwhile, make the filling. In a large mixing bowl, whisk the eggs until frothy, then gradually add the sugar. When the mixture is a lemon-yellow colour, add the lemon zest and gently fold in the juice. Sift the flour and baking powder into the egg mixture and fold together until combined.

5 Pour the filling over the hot crust and return it to the oven to cook for 25 minutes. When cooked, let the slice cool completely in the pan before dusting with icing sugar. Cut into squares with a sharp knife before turning out.

Makes at least 24

Whenever I drop in on Lil, the first place I head for is her backyard, where a very generous lemon tree hangs over the neighbour's fence. It seems that for half the year this beautiful tree bears luscious, juicy lemons. The scent of freshly zested lemons energises me, and I find it always cleanses a kitchen of any heavy cooking odours.

These sweet but tangy cakes make for the ultimate afternoon-tea delicacy. Served with a good cup of Earl Grey in a delicate tea set, they always make me salivate. They won't rise much when cooked because of all that yummy butter and almond meal, but they're great for the gluten-intolerant.

Method

1 Preheat the oven to 180˚C.

2 Cream the butter and sugar together until light and fluffy, then add the eggs one at a time, mixing between each addition. Add the lemon zest, two-thirds of the lemon juice and the vanilla and beat until combined (the mixture will look slightly curdled due to the lemon juice). Add the polenta, almond meal and coconut and combine.

3 Spoon generous tablespoons into a muffin tray lined with two patty pans per hole (a double layer of patty pans gives the cakes a better shape). Bake for 12–15 minutes or until slightly golden.

4 Mix the icing sugar with the remaining lemon juice and spread over the cooled cakes.

Makes 18

Ingredients

260 g butter
1¼ cups caster sugar
4 eggs
finely grated zest and
  juice of 3 lemons
1 teaspoon vanilla extract
130 g polenta
130 g almond meal
130 g shredded coconut
300 g icing sugar

Last year Lil, Atticus and I were all living together again in the lead-up to my wedding to Simon. I had just returned from a trip to Italy to find Lil, who leads a fairly hectic life at the best of times, surrounded with boxes and suitcases. She announced she was off to Europe for three months to work the summer festivals with a stilt troupe, and she was attempting to pack her costumes, which included a giant kangaroo suit and an Aussie surf-lifesaver uniform each weighing about 25 kilos.

To complicate things further, she planned to move to the apartment above my shop on her return. So, as she frantically packed her whole life into various categories, I felt the need to nurture my girl. I was excited for her, a little sad for me, and curious, to say the least, as to what the customs officers would think of the contents of her luggage. Once again we pack and shift, but we are never too far from one another.

The night before Lil left, various members of the clan wanted to say goodbye, so I thought the simple, fresh flavours of a homely roast chicken would be just perfect.

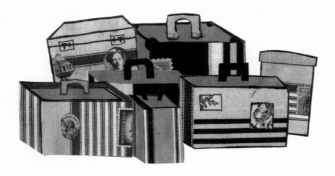

Serves 8

Roast Chicken with Marjoram & Parsley Butter & Heavenly Baked Potatoes

This recipe uses the classic French method of stuffing a chicken between the flesh and the skin. It can be tricky the first time you do it but the results are worth it. The key is to gently separate the skin from the flesh without tearing it. I find the best way to do this is to hold the chook with one hand at its bottom end, then gently insert your fingers between the skin and the flesh as if you were putting on a pair of gloves.

This is a meal fit for a last supper. The night before Lil's departure we had quite a crowd at our place, but you could easily halve these quantities for a weeknight dinner.

Ingredients

100 g butter

8 cloves garlic, finely chopped with ½ teaspoon salt and ½ teaspoon sugar to make a paste

1 bunch marjoram, leaves picked and finely chopped

1 bunch flat-leaf parsley, leaves picked and finely chopped

olive oil, for cooking

2 leeks, trimmed and well washed, thickly sliced

2 large organic chickens, rinsed and dried with paper towel

sea salt and freshly ground black pepper

10 large potatoes, sliced in half lengthways, then each half turned face-down and sliced diagonally at 2 mm intervals, taking care not to cut all the way through

2 bunches baby carrots, tops trimmed to 5 mm, peeled

2 tablespoons plain flour

½ cup white wine

Method

1 Melt the butter with the garlic paste in a saucepan over low heat. As soon as the butter has melted, remove the pan from the heat and add the herbs. Mix well then set aside – it should cool and solidify. Preheat the oven to 220°C.

2 Line a large deep baking dish with foil. Drizzle a little olive oil into the dish and toss in the leeks, lightly coating them in oil.

3 Gently separate the chicken skin from the flesh with your hands, then take a spoonful of the herb butter and push it as far as you can under the skin and around all the joints, rubbing it into the flesh. Keep going till you've used half the butter, then turn the chook over and repeat on the other side, reserving just a small amount. Seal the neck end by pulling the skin over and under and tucking it between the wings, and the other end by pushing the parson's nose inside the opening.

4 Place the chicken on top of the leeks in the baking dish and rub the remaining herb butter over the outside of the chicken. Sprinkle with salt and pepper then bake for 20 minutes.

5 Line a baking dish with greaseproof paper and place the potatoes in the dish, flat-side down. Brush them with a little olive oil then sprinkle with salt and pepper.

6 Remove the chicken and leeks from the oven and baste with the roasting juices using a pastry brush or turkey baster. Return to the oven with the potatoes and cook for 20 minutes. Remove the chicken and leeks from the oven again and baste. Place the carrots around the chicken and coat with any roasting juices. Return to the oven for a further 15 minutes.

7 Remove the chicken and leeks from the oven and test the meat by carefully inserting the tip of a sharp knife into the thickest part of the leg, then tipping the chicken to allow the juices to run into the pan. If the juices are clear, the bird is cooked, but if not baste one more time and return it to the oven. Depending on how well-cooked you like your veggies, either pull them out now and set aside or leave them in with the chicken to cook some more.

8 Once the chicken is cooked, remove from the oven, transfer to a large serving dish and surround with the carrots and leeks. Cover with foil and leave to stand while you make the gravy.

9 Pour some of the roasting juices from the pan into a cup. In a small bowl, mix the flour with 2 tablespoons of the juices and the wine. Stir into a paste, making sure there are no lumps. Pour the remaining juices into a heavy-based pan, add the flour mixture and 1 cup water and stir over medium heat. Reduce the gravy for a few minutes until the consistency is to your liking then season with a little salt and pepper.

10 Stack the potatoes in a bowl or on a serving platter. Uncover the chicken and vegetables and place on the table, ready to be carved. Pour the gravy into a jug and serve separately.

Bon Appétit!

Mussels à la Chez Janou

I'm wild about basil; it's always been one of my favourite herbs. I regularly make pesto and use it not just as a pasta sauce but also as a topping for vegetables or as a salad dressing. I learnt of another way to serve it one night while dining at Chez Janou, a ridiculously charming little bistro in Paris. A plate of bubbling mussels in pesto had just been whisked past me, the aroma of basil lingering long after they had gone. Impulsively I ordered this little entrée as a main course and devoured every one of the plump morsels, and then came back the next night for a repeat performance.

Ingredients

- 1 kg fresh mussels (the small black ones), lightly scrubbed with steel wool
- 3 bay leaves
- 1 teaspoon whole peppercorns
- ½ bunch fresh flat-leaf parsley, leaves finely chopped
- ½ bottle Riesling or other dry white wine
- 1 quantity Pesto (see page 7)

Method

1 Place the mussels, bay leaves, peppercorns, parsley, wine and 3 cups water in a large pot with a lid. Cover and bring to the boil, simmering for about 5 minutes or until all the mussels open.

2 Remove from the heat and drain the mussels in a colander, discarding the herbs, flavourings and cooking liquid. Let the mussels cool and discard any that haven't opened. Break off the empty half of the shell and carefully remove the beard from the flesh (I find a little pair of nail scissors very handy for this job).

3 Line a baking tray with foil and, working in batches, lay out the mussels flesh-side up, keeping them close together. Spoon a large teaspoonful of pesto into each mussel.

4 Place the tray under a medium grill for about 2 minutes or until the pesto is golden. (Keep your eyes on them as they can burn very quickly, and as the mussels have already been cooked you don't want them to dry out.) Repeat with the remaining mussels. Serve as they are for a wonderful entrée, or if you're feeling adventurous toss them through your favourite cooked pasta (use 100 g dried pasta per person).

Serves 6 as an entrée

I'm not quite sure why it's called French toast, as I've been to France several times and never once had this there, nor have I seen a recipe for it in any French cookbook. As a child, my mother made this for us on special occasions, but now I never need a reason to make French toast – it's so delicious I have it whenever I can. They say it's good for you to eat a big breakfast and that your calorie intake should be at its highest in the morning, so I can't think of a better way to start the day. The thicker the slices of bread, the more delicious it is. If you are health-conscious, try using grainy, wholemeal bread instead of white. I always serve French toast with fresh berries and slices of lemon as it's an absolutely perfect combo.

Method

1 Whisk the eggs, milk and vanilla together in a mixing bowl.

2 Mix the cinnamon and sugar together and tip onto a small dinner plate.

3 Heat a teaspoon of butter in a frying pan over medium heat. Take a slice of bread and dip it into the egg mixture on both sides, letting it soak up the liquid for a few seconds, then quickly place in the frying pan. Cook on both sides until golden, then place onto the plate with the cinnamon and sugar and coat both sides.

4 Repeat with remaining bread slices and serve just as they are cooked with fresh strawberries and lemon slices.

Serves 6

Ingredients

2 eggs

2 cups milk

1 teaspoon
vanilla extract

½ teaspoon cinnamon

½ cup sugar

40 g butter

6 thick slices bread
(French stick
is perfect)

1 punnet fresh
strawberries

1 lemon, sliced

LETTER FROM LIL: I'm sitting here in the sweltering heat of Puerto Escondido, a beachside town that feels a world away from any other part of Mexico. It's funny, every town Mon Chew and I go to is so distinctly different – there are often no similarities at all except for the food. Ah, the food! When we first arrived, the difficulties of not speaking the language relegated us to pointing to things or ordering familiar dishes such as tacos and enchiladas. However, after three or four experiences eating deep-fried chicken tacos with lashings of slightly-off sour cream, we decided that we really should be more adventurous.

So, as a result we've tried *birria*, stewed goat salted and cooked for hours, served with lime, jalapeños and chilli, and *pozole*, a delicious soup with hominy beans, served with a salad of radishes, lettuce and onion tipped in and mixed through the soup. We've also had a stewed chicken dish called *chichirria* (or something similar) that takes eight hours to cook and is served with tortillas and lime, jalapeños and chilli.

We ate incredibly well in the town of San Miguel de Allende, except for the pork. We arrived there after a very long bus trip and I was tired, hungry and grumpy. Unfortunately we ended up at a tourist hub that served 'Mexican specialities'. I ordered soup, and Mon Chew ordered what purported to be pork and beans, but something must have got lost in translation, as she ended up with green slime and a brown purée that vaguely resembled beans. Served, funnily enough, with lime, jalapeños and chilli. We both tried a little and soon felt decidedly ill – we might stick with deep-fried tacos after all . . .

Guacamole

When it comes to guacamole, I am very pedantic (in fact, I'd go so far as to say I'm a pain in the *tamale*). There are certain no-nos that I just will not tolerate: added oil, cream of any kind, tomatoes or other random vegetables or nuts. Fresh chillies must always be used, and on no account should the guacamole be baked. Sometimes necessity will overrule, but try not to deviate from the true Mexican guacamole – it's perfect! I love to add the finely chopped roots of the coriander as well as the leaves as they add a strong, nutty flavour, but this part is optional.

Avocado is the only fruit that contains fat, so no more needs to be added here. The Mexicans use lime juice to counteract this fattiness and preserve the amazing colour of the avocado flesh. If using guacamole as a topping for nachos, melt the cheese over the nachos first, then put a generous scoop of guacamole on top followed by sour cream, sweet chilli sauce and fresh coriander. Guacamole is also perfect served simply on individual witlof leaves.

Method

1 Cut the avocados in half, remove the seeds and scoop all the flesh into a bowl. Squeeze the lime juice over (if the limes are very firm, put them in the microwave on a medium setting for about 8 seconds to make them juicier).

2 Add the chopped chilli, garlic, onion, chopped coriander leaves and roots (if using) and mix together with a fork (take care not to over-mash as guacamole should have a chunky texture). Season and serve as a dip with flatbreads or corn chips, with nachos, or with corn fritters and crispy bacon for a delicious light meal.

Makes about 2 cups

Ingredients

4 ripe but firm avocados

juice of 2 or 3 limes

1 red or green chilli, finely chopped and deseeded (you can add more if you're feeling brave)

2 cloves garlic, finely chopped with 1 teaspoon salt to make a paste

½ red onion, finely chopped

½ bunch coriander, leaves picked and chopped, roots cleaned and finely chopped (roots optional)

sea salt and freshly ground black pepper, to taste

Chilli Con Carne

This classic dish can be so much more than just 'chilli with meat'. It's the perfect dish to serve at a party as it can be made a couple of days in advance and frozen (its flavour improves after a day or so). Just remember to leave enough time to let it thaw properly before you reheat it.

I love a Mexican-themed party – it's a chance to wear too much colour, roast a small pig and throw back an unwise number of Margaritas. Served as a main course with steamed brown rice, this dish is perfect to help soak up a little of that Mexican cheer.

I like to use fresh chillies and add them to the *soffrito* mixture (the gently fried onion and garlic) to soften their kick just slightly. For diehard chilli fans, the addition of jalapeños at the end give a more authentic Mexican flavour. Modern Mexican cuisine has become quite rich but I think if you go back to basics and don't overdo dishes – by adding cream, for example – you'll be singing *Guantanamera* in no time.

Ingredients

¼ cup olive oil
2 large onions, finely chopped
4 cloves garlic, finely chopped with 1 teaspoon salt to make a paste
1 large red capsicum, white insides and seeds removed, finely diced
1–2 small red chillies, deseeded and rinsed under cold water, finely chopped
250 g veal mince
250 g beef mince
250 g pork mince
1 bay leaf
1 tablespoon maple syrup
2 × 400 g cans diced tomatoes
70 g tomato paste
½ cup beef stock
1 × 750 g can red kidney beans
1½ tablespoons sliced jalapeño peppers in vinegar (optional)
sea salt and freshly ground black pepper
steamed brown rice, to serve

Method

1 Heat 2 tablespoons of the olive oil in a large, heavy-based frying pan over medium heat. Add the onions and fry for 5 minutes, then add the garlic paste and stir through. Add the diced capsicum and cook for 3–4 minutes, then add the finely chopped chillies. Stir, turn the heat to low and continue to cook – the *soffrito* will turn a rich red colour.

2 Meanwhile, in a heavy-based pan with a lid, heat the remaining olive oil over high heat then add all the meat, breaking it up with a wooden spoon to blend. As soon as you hear the meat sizzling, turn the heat down to medium, add the bay leaf, cover and cook for 10 minutes, stirring occasionally. Uncover and carefully tip out any excess water, then return the mince to the heat and stir through the maple syrup and the *soffrito*. Reduce the heat to low, cover and cook for 10 minutes.

3 Add the tomatoes, tomato paste and beef stock, mix well then cover and cook for 15 minutes. Stir through the kidney beans and jalapeños (if using), season to taste and cook for a further 15 minutes before serving with steamed brown rice.

Serves 6

Chicken Enchiladas

Mrs Beaver was my tour manager and PA, as well as my son Atticus's beloved nanny for nearly 5 years when he was small. Her real name is Katrina, but we christened her Mrs Beaver early on as she was so industrious and efficient – constantly beavering about to make our lives easier. She came on tour with us and would throw herself into any task: painting props, setting up the stage, driving the van – she'd even remember everyone's birthday. At the end of a busy day, she'd send us off for a long bath and whip up something heavenly, like these enchiladas, for dinner.

This rich cheesy recipe could sit equally well in the comfort-food section, as it's perfect for a cold winter's night. The enchiladas are at least 4 cm thick, so you'll need a reasonably deep baking dish to hold them.

Method

1 Preheat the oven to 180°C. In a heavy-based saucepan, fry the onions in the olive oil over low heat. When they become translucent, add the crushed garlic and cook for a few minutes.

2 Add the spinach, cumin, nutmeg, salt and pepper to the pan. Cook for 2–3 minutes then transfer to a bowl, letting the mixture cool for 5 minutes. Fold in the shredded chicken and sour cream.

3 Lightly butter a rectangular or oval-shaped baking dish and spoon in half the béchamel sauce in a layer. Place one piece of lavash bread flat on a dinner plate and spoon a generous amount (about 3 heaped tablespoons) of the chicken mixture on the end closest to you. Roll up the enchilada and place it seam-side down in the dish. Repeat with the rest of the ingredients to make eight enchiladas (if you're using an oval dish you may have to cut two in half).

4 Spread the remaining béchamel over, sprinkle with grated cheese then season with salt and pepper and a little sprinkle of nutmeg. Bake for 30–40 minutes until golden. Serve one enchilada per person as they're quite rich.

Serves 8

Ingredients

2 brown onions, finely chopped

2 tablespoons olive oil

2 cloves garlic, crushed

2 × 250 g packets frozen spinach, thawed and drained

1 teaspoon ground cumin

½ teaspoon ground nutmeg, plus extra for sprinkling

sea salt and freshly ground black pepper

1 barbecued chicken, meat shredded

1 cup sour cream

2–3 cups Béchamel (see page 6)

8 pieces lavash or mountain bread

2 cups grated cheddar cheese

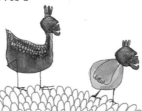

Italia

The last time I visited Italy was on my honeymoon, or 'familymoon' as we renamed it. My husband Simon and I were married in New York at the end of 2008, and we then set off for Italy together with three of our six kids. It was the dead of winter, which meant few tourists, cold nights, roaring fires and falling snow.

I had been to Tuscany many times but never to Le Marche, the magnificent area surrounding the Siblini mountains. A 200-year-old house perched proudly atop the tiny city of San Martino became our home for three glorious weeks. Le Marche is known for its exquisite produce, from pungent cheeses to sausages and aged prosciutto, but most of all it is famous for its truffles. We tried truffle pasta, truffle olive oil, truffle-infused cheese – even truffle honey.

Each night around the dinner table was a celebration of new flavours and a chance for us to recap our daily adventures. For three weeks, there were no distractions – no television, no newspapers, no financial reports or political gloom and doom. Surrounded by the natural beauty of the snow-covered mountains and the antiquity of this elegant country, my children were well and truly swept up in the magic of Italy.

I had this dish – one of my favourite pasta meals of all time – in a little restaurant in the Trastevere district of Rome in 1988. Half the excitement of that meal was the wonderful adventure it was to get there. My then-husband Julian and I wound our way through the narrow streets and across the Tiber with Lil, Atticus and our nanny Mrs Beaver (who was always delighted to go on a culinary expedition). We'd been sightseeing all day and were weary and very hungry. Our exhausted little group was greeted at the restaurant by the owner/chef/maître d extraordinaire, who enthusiastically insisted that the only thing worth eating there that night were the leftovers. I happen to be a big fan of leftovers, so we willingly agreed, and we weren't disappointed.

Whether you have some cooked sausages, a bit of last night's meatloaf or maybe just some extra bacon in the fridge, this pasta is all about using up leftovers – it's Italy's answer to bubble and squeak. The one thing that remains constant is the addition of fresh ricotta, stirred through just before serving. These quantities are just a guide – I always make a big bowl of this with whatever I have to hand.

Method

1 Bring two pans of salted water to a boil, one large and one small. Using tongs, carefully drop the tomatoes into the small pan of boiling water to blanch for about 3 minutes (the skins will split). Transfer the tomatoes to a bowl and leave to cool, then peel off the skins.

2 Throw the pasta in the large pan of boiling water, add a drizzle of olive oil and cook until al dente, then drain.

3 Meanwhile, in a large, heavy-based frying pan, fry the onions and celery or fennel in the olive oil over low heat until the onions are translucent. Add three-quarters of the crushed garlic, the sausage, chorizo and plenty of salt and pepper and cook for 5 minutes.

4 Chop the peeled tomatoes roughly and transfer all the flesh and juice to the onion mixture in the frying pan. Cook on a low heat for at least 10 minutes.

5 Drizzle some olive oil into a large serving bowl and add the rest of the crushed garlic, the parsley and the cooked pasta, tossing gently to lightly coat the pasta. Add the tomato mixture and gently crumble the fresh ricotta on top, then fold through. Sprinkle over some fresh parmesan, season generously with pepper and serve immediately.

Ingredients

6 vine-ripened tomatoes

500 g rigatoni pasta

2 large white or brown onions, chopped

2 sticks celery *or* 2 bulbs fennel, chopped

¼ cup olive oil, plus extra for drizzling

4 cloves garlic, crushed

4 large cooked sausages, cut into 2.5 cm slices

2 chorizos, cut into 2.5 cm slices

sea salt and freshly ground black pepper

large handful freshly chopped flat-leaf parsley

500 g fresh ricotta

1–2 cups freshly grated parmesan cheese

Serves 4

Artichokes

Of all the myriad vegetables you can find at your local greengrocer these days, the artichoke remains one of the most mysterious. Shaped like an overweight pine cone, I often wonder: who was the genius that discovered its hidden flesh?

During our 'familymoon' in Italy, our daughter Victoria curiously pointed to a very perky, proud bunch of artichokes at the local markets. 'What are they?' she asked. I was aghast that she had never tried them, so we bought a large bag and went home straight away to cook. That night, our rustic kitchen buzzing with anticipation, we steamed the artichokes and made a big bowl of aïoli to go with them. As we showed Victoria how to peel off each leaf, dip it into the aïoli then scrape the flesh against her teeth, her face erupted into sheer joy. From that day she was a true convert, and fresh artichokes became a constant on our holiday menu.

Ingredients

6 large fresh artichokes, trimmed and outer leaves removed

½ teaspoon salt

1 quantity aïoli (see Mayonnaise recipe on page 6)

Method

1 Place the artichokes in a large heavy-based saucepan and fill with water to a depth of 4 cm. Sprinkle with the salt, cover and cook over medium heat for 20 minutes.

2 Serve each steamed artichoke with a generous spoonful of aïoli. Place an empty bowl in the middle of the table for the scraped leaves. The artichoke heart is the jewel in the crown – slice it in half, remove any hair-like vegetation then smother it with more aïoli and enjoy!

Serves 6

Cortona Pasta for Pigsy

On a sparkling spring day, my husband Simon and I were wandering around the medieval streets of Cortona, a town in the Tuscany region. I had walked around this town before but had never ventured up the winding narrow paths to the very top of the hill, where a magnificent church and monastery command the best views of Tuscany. As we climbed, I was distracted by the ancient houses clinging to the hillside, nestled in amongst olive trees, wild herbs and poppies, and I noticed the healthiest patch of marjoram I've ever seen, growing out of a stone wall. I pilfered a decent-sized bunch, and that night created this pasta. It was so delicious that Simon had three helpings, which earned him his nickname of 'Pigsy'.

You'll need a bunch of marjoram for this recipe (about half a cup). This may seem like a lot, but it is an important element of this pasta sauce. Don't use dried marjoram as it has nowhere near the subtle, sweet flavour of the fresh herb.

Method

1 Bring two large pans of salted water to a boil. Using tongs, carefully drop the tomatoes into one of the pans of boiling water and blanch for about 3 minutes (the skins will split). Transfer the tomatoes to a bowl and leave to cool, then peel off the skins.

2 Throw the pasta into the other pan of boiling water, add a drizzle of olive oil and cook until al dente, then drain.

3 Meanwhile, heat a generous splash of olive oil in a heavy-based saucepan. Toss in the prosciutto and pancetta and cook for 5 minutes (if the meat sticks to the pan, turn the heat down a little). Add the garlic and a twist of pepper and cook for another 5 minutes, stirring occasionally.

4 Chop the tomatoes roughly and transfer all the flesh and juice to the pan. Stir well to combine the ingredients and simmer over medium heat for 5 minutes. Add the marjoram and cook for another 5 minutes, then taste for seasoning.

5 Serve the pasta in a large bowl with the sauce spooned over and a sprinkle of fresh parmesan on top.

Serves 4

Ingredients

14 medium-sized
  ripe tomatoes
500 g rigatoni pasta
olive oil, for cooking
170 g finely sliced prosciutto
90 g finely sliced pancetta
4 cloves garlic, crushed
freshly ground black pepper
½ cup fresh marjoram leaves
1 cup freshly grated
  parmesan cheese

Spain

When I left Spain in 2002 after a three-week stint working in Madrid, I was inconsolable. I had visited the city many times before, but going there on holiday was a whole different ball game to actually working and living there. Every day of that trip was so full of emotion; I learnt so much about the Spanish way of life and I felt so at home. On the plane back to Sydney, I scribbled out this note, trying to describe how I felt:

Enormous tears roll down my cheeks, heavy, like the rain that washed Madrid last night. Old Madrid is overwhelming, dripping with stories and secrets of bygone eras. And the flavours – the tartness of the goat's cheese that sends my jaw into spasms; the smooth jamón iberico *that makes you feel a part of this ancient culture of untamed emotions; the* pulpo, boquerones, morzillo y aros, manchego, membrillo *and wine from the Rioja. The deep-set eyes of the Madrileños, the husky voices of the women, their skin, so soft yet strong enough to endure the dry, torturous Iberian weather.*

My mind is sweeping over the last three weeks: Plaza Mejor, El Retiro, Tio Pepe, the Prado, the Museo del Jamón. In this place there is no ambivalence, only passion – conversations and hand gestures fiery and wild. My heart is now heavy, the smell of leather and tobacco still lingers. I am Spanish and proud.

GAZPACHO

This is my standard tomato-based gazpacho recipe. Some people don't bother peeling the tomatoes as they say the skins add flavour, but unless I've grown the tomatoes myself or they're certified organic, I remove the skin.

If you're making this soup for a special occasion, make sure you leave plenty of time to chill it, as adding ice to the gazpacho will dilute the flavour. And you might need to add more seasoning than you would for a hot soup – taste the finished dish to be sure.

Method

1 Bring a large pan of water to the boil then, using tongs, carefully drop the tomatoes in to blanch for about 3 minutes (until the skins have split). Transfer the tomatoes to a bowl and leave to cool, then peel off the skins and roughly chop.

2 Place the bread chunks in a large ceramic bowl and cover with water. Leave to soak for a couple of hours – the bread will swell and soften.

3 Squeeze any excess water from the bread chunks and place them in a blender or food processor with the garlic, salt, pepper and chilli. Give it a good whiz, add the tomatoes and whiz again until puréed, then pour half of this mixture back into the clean ceramic bowl.

4 Add the rest of the ingredients to the blender, whiz until puréed, then pour into the bowl and give it a good stir with a wooden spoon. Taste for seasoning and add more salt or pepper if required. Refrigerate for at least 2 hours, then serve in individual soup bowls.

Serves 8

Ingredients

10 large vine-ripened tomatoes

½ loaf stale white bread, crusts removed, bread torn into small chunks

2–3 cloves garlic, peeled

1 teaspoon sea salt

1 teaspoon freshly ground black pepper

1 bell pepper (small, mild chilli), finely chopped

2 small cucumbers, deseeded and roughly chopped

1 large red capsicum, white insides and seeds removed, roughly chopped

3 spring onions, roughly chopped

2 sticks celery, roughly chopped

⅓ cup sherry vinegar

⅓ cup olive oil

pinch paprika

AJO BLANCO
(WHITE GAZPACHO)

Almonds are one of my favourite nuts, so when I first tried this cold, creamy soup I thought I'd died and gone to heaven. The Spanish often float fruit in their cold soups and the addition of frozen muscat grapes to this not only keeps the soup really cold, but the sweet grapes explode in your mouth and combine with the more savoury ingredients to create a symphony of flavours. I have also used blueberries or rockmelon in place of the grapes and both are scrumptious.

Ingredients

½ loaf stale white bread, crusts removed, bread torn into small chunks

300 g blanched almonds

⅓ cup olive oil

1 teaspoon ground white pepper

⅓ cup sherry vinegar

3 cloves garlic, finely chopped with 1 teaspoon salt and 1 teaspoon sugar to make a paste

1 generous bunch (at least 300 g) muscat grapes or sweet seedless grapes

Method

1 Place the bread chunks in a large ceramic bowl and cover with water. Leave to soak for a couple of hours – the bread will swell and soften.

2 Put the almonds, oil, pepper and vinegar in a blender or food processor and blend to a thick paste. Add the garlic paste to the blender with a little cold water and give it a good whiz.

3 Squeeze any excess water from the bread chunks and add them to the blender, processing to a smooth, creamy soup. Taste for seasoning and add more salt or pepper if required, then chill for at least 2 hours.

4 Meanwhile, place the grapes in the freezer for 2 hours.

5 Just before serving, remove the soup from the fridge and give it a good stir. Place a handful of frozen grapes in each soup bowl, cover with a generous ladle of soup and serve.

Serves 6–8

This is my mum Margot's recipe for *soplillos*. They are burst-in-your-mouth, slightly malty, nutty meringues that are a family favourite. Whenever my mum sends me a recipe there is always a little bonus tip attached – after years of cooking for a big family there's not much she doesn't know. When she sent me this one, there was a little note in the top right-hand corner of the page that read 'an average eggwhite is equivalent to 2 tablespoons'. I'd never have known that, and would certainly never have thought to measure an eggwhite!

Method

1 Preheat the oven to 150°C.

2 Roast the almonds on a large baking tray for about 10 minutes or until golden brown. Leave to cool then pulse in a food processor until they are about the size of pine nuts.

3 Beat the eggwhites and the salt together until they are stiff and snowy, then gradually beat in the sugar until the mixture becomes very stiff and shiny. Add the lemon juice and zest, and gently fold in the almonds.

4 Cover three baking trays with greaseproof paper (put a little dot of meringue mixture between the tray and the paper to hold it in place). Form the meringues using two spoons and place evenly onto the trays, then bake for 30 minutes.

5 To make these really special, you could dip them in melted chocolate before serving. When the meringues have cooled completely, melt the chocolate chips in a heatproof bowl that fits snugly over a saucepan of boiling water, or cook in the microwave on the highest setting for 30 seconds, stir, and cook for another 30 seconds until melted (watch it like a hawk so it doesn't burn). Dunk one half of each meringue in the chocolate, letting them dry on a rack before serving.

Makes about 36 small meringues or 24 big ones

Ingredients

400 g whole blanched almonds

6 medium-sized eggwhites

pinch salt

500 g caster sugar

juice and finely grated zest of an unwaxed lemon

½ cup dark chocolate chips, optional

MARGOT'S FLAN

In 2002 I was in Madrid working on my TV show for the Playhouse Disney channel. We were to shoot twenty-five episodes in ten days with a crew of thirty or so non-English-speaking, cigarette-toting Spaniards. I was a little worried about the language barrier, so I invited my mother, Margot, along in the hope that she could perhaps shed a little light on the technical directions that we would be given. She hung around for the first few days, completely charmed the crew, made sure we knew what the words for 'action', 'cut' and 'repeat that take' were in Spanish, then left us to catch up with all her old buddies who she hadn't seen in almost fifty years.

Each night, after a twelve-hour day of filming, I'd return to my hotel room to discover my mother had amassed an array of every Spanish delicacy Madrid had to offer. All her friends from every corner of Spain had brought her home-coming gifts of food. This included charcuterie of every persuasion, pickled vegetables, salted almonds and delicious pastries and flans made from unim-aginable amounts of egg yolk and sugar. The chest of drawers that once held my clothes now displayed a fine array of blood sausage and pungent cheeses. As soon as I opened the door each night, there she would be, wielding some little Madrileñian morsel for me to try.

We certainly ate some amazing food on that trip, but the dessert flan my mother made one night was definitely the highlight – everything else paled in comparison. It was the best flan I've ever tried, so rich and unbelievably creamy. A Spanish flan is more like a crème caramel than a pastry with fruit. Don't be horrified by the ingredients – nine egg yolks is nothing in the scheme of things and, just think, you'll have enough eggwhites left over for a decent batch of meringues!

Flan can be served cold or at room temperature. If I'm making this for a dinner party, I put it in the oven just before I serve the first course, then turn the oven off just as I'm serving the second course, and the flan is usually the perfect temperature to serve for dessert. Play around with the timings yourself – you'll soon see what works best. If the flan has been chilled, dip the flan dish in a pan of hot water to loosen it before turning it out.

Method

1 Preheat the oven to 180°C.

2 In a medium-sized bowl, whisk the egg yolks, vanilla, half the sugar and the evaporated milk together until all the ingredients are combined and the sugar has completely dissolved.

3 Pour the other cup of sugar into a saucepan and heat, stirring gently, until it starts to bubble and caramelise (it will turn into a deep-golden syrup), brushing down the sides of the pan with a wet pastry brush as you go.

4 When the sugar has completely caramelised, pour it into a round, ovenproof dish and carefully tip the dish from side to side so that the caramel covers the entire base. Let it cool for 5 minutes, then place the dish inside a deep roasting tin and fill the tin with water to come halfway up the outside of the dish.

5 Give the egg mixture a light whisk then pour it into the dish on top of the caramel. Place on the middle shelf of the oven and bake for 45 minutes.

6 Check the flan, and if the top is solid but spongy, turn off the heat and let it cool in the oven. If not, continue cooking for another 5–10 minutes until it has set, then cool in the oven as before. This is perfect served at room temperature or can be refrigerated overnight and served the next day.

Serves 8

Ingredients

9 egg yolks

1 teaspoon vanilla extract

2 cups sugar

1 × 400 ml can evaporated milk

New York

I ♥ DUCK & JICAMA SALAD

My mother Margot is famous in our family for growing weird and wonderful vegetables, and one of her favourites is the jicama, although she calls it a *singkamas* (as they do in the Philippines). It's like a cross between a radish, a cucumber and a potato, and it can be fried, steamed or used raw in salads. In the Philippines, they slice it and eat it fresh with salt. Here, you'll find jicama in Asian grocers if you don't happen to have any growing in the backyard.

On the final day of a recent visit to New York, I made a last-minute trek to my favourite little diner, The Habana Cafe. As it was filled to the gills, I got a blood orange, mango, duck and jicama salad to take away, and ate it in the cab on the way to the airport – it was heavenly. When I returned home, I was inspired to start experimenting with this interesting vegetable. It is chameleon-like, with a humble taste that takes on the flavours of any other ingredient it accompanies, whilst providing a juicy, crunchy texture. If you can't find jicama, substitute with long cucumber.

Ingredients

1 jicama, peeled and cut into thin strips

1 orange, peeled, pith and seeds removed, flesh roughly chopped

1 bunch watercress or snowpea shoots, any woody stems removed

1 cup mint leaves, roughly chopped, plus extra leaves to garnish

1 Chinese roast duck, skin and bones removed, meat shredded *or* 500 g roast or smoked chicken meat

1 mango, peeled and sliced

Dressing

1 tablespoon rice wine vinegar

1 tablespoon fish sauce

¼ cup caster sugar

1 teaspoon finely grated ginger

1 tablespoon tamarind purée, dissolved in 1 tablespoon water

2 finely chopped chillies

sea salt and freshly ground black pepper

Method

1 To make the dressing, combine all the ingredients and whisk with a fork.

2 Place all the salad ingredients in a large bowl and pour the dressing over the top. Gently toss everything together and serve on a large platter garnished with a generous handful of mint.

Serves 4

RICE REG & CAROL'S PUDDING

England

LETTER FROM LIL: After the challenges of Mexico, I have not felt at all daunted by Europe's culinary offerings. I love all the cheeses and have devoured more than my annual intake in just three days in France. I've drunk steins of beer in Munich to wash down the satisfying saltiness of a pretzel that was the width of my hips. I've even tried the dense, starch-filled *pierogi*, the Polish dumpling that exists solely to soak up the excess apple and cherry vodka that keeps you warm in winter.

At the moment I'm travelling with two English boys, Sid and Sean, and we're using Sid's parents' place at Abingdon-on-Thames near Oxford as our base, in between trips to the Continent. It is hard to describe the warm welcome I received from the lovely Reg and Carol Sidlow. Reg is a classic English gentleman who enjoys bell-ringing and always has a good story to tell. Carol is wonderfully easy-going and is forever producing delicious food in vast quantities, helping my waistband to become just that little bit tighter every day.

Yesterday, after yet another glorious meal, a traditional rice pudding was served, and after just one bite I asked for the recipe. All three Sidlows chipped in with some advice: the best garnish to use, the perfect amount of milk to add, the best way to stop the milk boiling over – this was obviously a treasured family favourite. Perhaps I enjoyed it all the more as I'll never forget the good company and satisfaction of my first rice-pudding experience.

Method

1 Preheat the oven to 200°C. Mix all the ingredients together and place in a small round or oval-shaped baking dish at least 4 cm deep.

2 Place the dish on a baking tray to prevent any messy spills, and bake for 1 hour (checking every 15–20 minutes and giving it a stir to prevent the rice sticking to the pan and becoming lumpy). A brown skin will appear on top of the pudding; you can stir this in or leave as is for a caramelised flavour. Serve with fresh strawberries or, as Sid recommends, a dollop of jam.

Serves 4

Ingredients

½ cup short-grain rice
2 tablespoons sugar
800 ml milk
pinch freshly grated or
  ground nutmeg
fresh strawberries or
  a dollop of jam, to serve

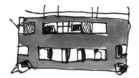

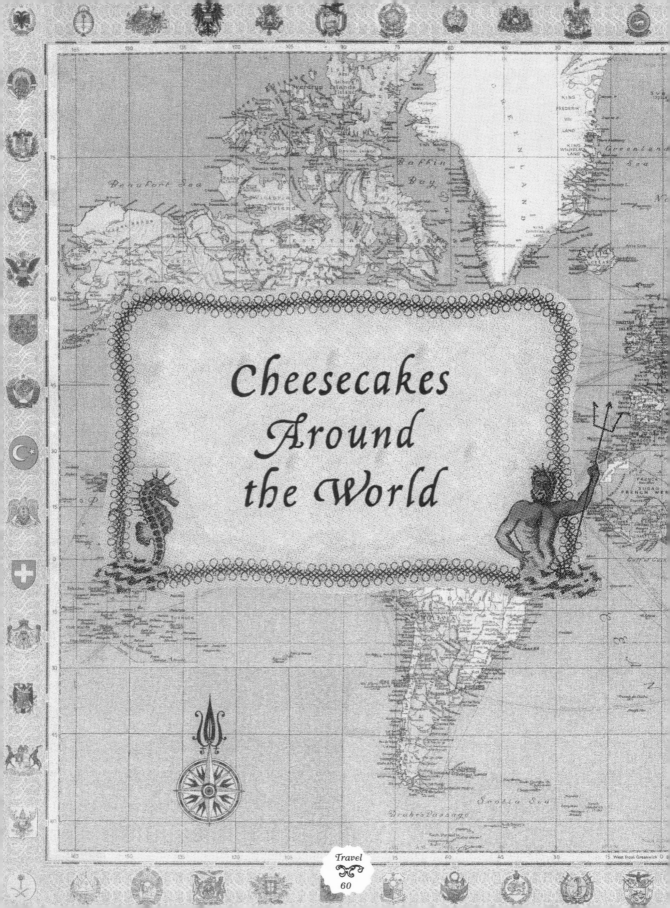

Cheesecakes Around the World

LETTER FROM LIL: For as long as I can remember, we would have a cheesecake made by my grandmother or one of my aunts at our family get-togethers. It always looked rich and delightful, but it never really interested me. Maybe this was due to the inevitable 24 egg yolks it contained (the Spanish never skimp on ingredients), or maybe my sweet tooth just hadn't developed back then. This all changed a couple of years ago when Meredith, who then lived above my mother's shop, brought me home a piece of baked ricotta cheesecake from one of Sydney's best *pasticcerias* that literally changed my life – it was dense and full of flavour, yet fluffy and light. Gone forever was the stodgy image of cheesecakes from my mind...

After this epiphany, cheesecake became my obsession, and on a subsequent trip to Europe I attempted to eat a piece of cheesecake in just about every town. First stop, London. I had kept to my £20-a-day budget and decided that a piece of cherry-topped cheesecake and a cappuccino would be in order. The cake was disappointingly gelatinous yet it soothed my jet-lagged throat and helped disguise the taste of the caffeinated dishwater that went with it.

The next piece I tried was in a tapas bar in Bristol. After gorging on meatballs and seafood the cake was an afterthought, but orange-chocolate cheesecake was too hard to resist. The crust was made from chocolate chips, and the jaffa swirl that ran through the middle led to a light yet creamy top that left a lovely, citrussy taste in my mouth. Then, back to London – I was en route to the airport to catch a 5 a.m. flight to Spain when I decided that a good meal and a glass of wine was in order, followed by cheesecake, of course. The plain unadulterated slice came with raspberry sauce and cream on the side, which I poured over rather too generously in my slightly inebriated state. Every mouthful of this perfectly simple cheesecake was savoured: its thin crust, subtly flavoured with nutmeg, never interfering with the light creamy texture of the filling.

Surprisingly, the Continent proved a bit of a disappointment for me, cheesecake-wise, probably because I was sidetracked by other things. In France, the cheese alone was just about all I could bear (almost consuming a wheel of Camembert per day), and in Munich I was distracted by the fabulous beer. The baked cheesecake I had in Madrid was unbearably rich in the 38°C heat – it prompted flashbacks of the 24-egg-yolk numbers I had avoided as a child. And I couldn't find one for love nor money in Croatia (although there was a surfeit of chocolate mousse).

This quest for the perfect cheesecake continued on the plane trip home, when I was pleasantly surprised to discover a slice hiding under the plastic lid of a container on my meal tray. The cake turned out to be disappointingly grainy (and still partly frozen), but I ate it anyway; it takes a lot to stop me, and I had just crossed nine time zones.

When I got back I found that my mama had heard about my cheesecake exploits and had been working furiously to try and master the perfect crust. She baked me a welcome-home cheesecake that knocked my socks off, and so now I turn to her whenever I need a fix. It's the variations that make them wonderful. The most recent was a delicious chocolate and ginger one that melted in my mouth – rich and mysterious with a gingery warmth, I knew I was home.

Baked Cheesecake

This is a good old-fashioned baked cheesecake based on one of my Grandma Mary's recipes. I love recipes that are handed down and developed further for the next generation to enjoy. Make it with pride, and hand it down to someone who'll hopefully make it for you one day.

Baking cheesecakes is an art form, and the secret is to knowing when to turn off the oven to let it cool (and not to repeatedly open the oven door to peek!). A bit of trial and error, and you'll perfect it in no time.

Ingredients

Crust

2 × 250 g packets plain sweet biscuits, such as Nice
1 teaspoon ground cinnamon
1 teaspoon ground nutmeg
135 g melted butter

Filling

500 g cream cheese
1 cup sugar
5 eggs
1 tablespoon vanilla extract
finely grated zest of 1 lemon

Topping

¼ cup sugar
1 teaspoon vanilla extract
300 ml sour cream
1 cup sour cherries, figs, blueberries or raspberries, to serve (optional)

Method

1 To make the crust, crush the biscuits in a food processor to a fine crumb, then add the cinnamon and nutmeg. Add the melted butter and process until well combined. Press half the mixture into the base of a 24 cm springform pan and the other half around the sides, making sure the crust is an even thickness. Refrigerate for at least 30 minutes while you make the filling.

2 Preheat the oven to 170°C. In a small mixing bowl, beat the cream cheese until soft. Gradually add the sugar, stirring between additions, and continue to stir while adding one egg at a time. As soon as all the eggs are mixed in, add the vanilla and the lemon zest, then pour this mixture into the chilled crust.

3 Bake for approximately 30 minutes, then test the cheesecake and if it is still very runny, bake for another 5 minutes. When the filling is almost set (but still slightly wobbly), turn the oven off and leave the cheesecake to cool in the oven. You'll find it is baked perfectly by the time it reaches room temperature.

4 While the cheesecake is cooling, make the topping by beating together the sugar, vanilla and the sour cream. Once the cheese-cake has cooled, spread this mixture evenly over the top, and use to fill any cracks on the surface. Remove the springform pan and top with fruit, if using.

Serves 10

Munich Cheesecake

My Grandma Mary has been making this cheesecake for decades, and whenever I ask her where she found the original recipe she waves her hand in the direction of her bookshelf, which holds hundreds of copies of *Gourmet*, *Epicure* and *Vogue Entertaining* – you name it, if it's a cooking magazine, she's subscribed to it. I think that's half the reason she is such a fabulous cook – at 101 years old, she is still poring over the latest glossies and comparing dishes. I often receive a recipe from her in the mail in her unmistakable handwriting, and I look forward to cooking whatever she has discovered. This recipe makes a small cheesecake but it's so rich you only need a sliver. The crunchy topping is what makes it so special.

This cake can be made a day or two before it is needed and also freezes well.

Method

1 Preheat the oven to 180°C. To make the crust, sift the flour, sugar and salt together into a bowl. Cut the butter into the flour using a pastry cutter or two knives (or I often rub the butter into the flour with my fingers just until it looks mealy). Stir the egg yolk into the mixture with a fork and knead lightly into a dough. Press this evenly over the base of a 24 cm springform pan and bake for about 20 minutes, or until golden brown, then remove from the oven and leave to cool (keeping the oven on at 180°C).

2 For the filling, beat the eggs and sugar together until thick and lemon-coloured. Add the cream cheese, salt and vanilla and beat until smooth. Spread the mixture over the cooled crust, then bake for a further 20 minutes. Remove from the oven and leave to cool again.

3 Meanwhile, prepare the topping. In a small saucepan over low heat, mix together the poppy seeds, raisins, sugar, milk, lemon zest and vanilla. Cook for at least 15 minutes, stirring frequently, until the mixture is thick but spreadable. Let the mixture cool to room temperature, then pour over the cooled cheesecake filling and spread evenly.

4 Preheat the grill to medium. Mix the brown sugar, flour and butter together to make coarse crumbs, and sprinkle over the topping. Place under the grill (about 15 cm away from the heat) until golden brown. Chill for a few hours, then remove the springform pan before serving.

Serves 10

Ingredients

Crust
1 cup plain flour
3 tablespoons sugar
¼ teaspoon salt
125 g butter
1 egg yolk

Filling
2 eggs, beaten
½ cup sugar
340 g cream cheese
¼ teaspoon salt
1 teaspoon vanilla extract

Topping
1 cup coarsely ground
  poppy seeds
¾ cup plump golden raisins
¾ cup sugar
½ cup milk
finely grated zest of 1 lemon
1 teaspoon vanilla extract
½ cup brown sugar
½ cup plain flour
60 g butter

Strawberry Cheesecake

I love fresh strawberries and the way they stain any ingredient you team them with a lovely pink hue. This recipe is tangy and light but full-bodied in flavour, and its striking colour makes it a beautiful dessert to serve with a dinner party. As you can make it the night before, it takes a little pressure off the host.

Ingredients

Crust

350 g crushed digestive biscuits (McVities wheat biscuits are perfect)

90 g crushed ginger snaps (the Swedish variety if you can find them)

1 cup roasted almonds, crushed

1 teaspoon ground cinnamon

120 g melted butter

Filling

½ cup icing sugar

500 g strawberries, hulled and cut into quarters

finely grated zest of 1 orange

½ cup Licor 43 liqueur or Cointreau

1 × 85 g packet strawberry jelly crystals

500 g cream cheese

2 egg yolks

¼ cup caster sugar

1 teaspoon vanilla extract

6 passionfruit, cut in half, pulp extracted

300 ml cream whipped with ¼ cup caster sugar

white chocolate curls, to serve (optional)

Method

1 The night before making this cheesecake, sift the icing sugar over the strawberries in a bowl and mix in the orange zest. Pour over the liqueur and chill in the fridge overnight.

2 To make the crust, place the dry ingredients in a food processor and pulse until finely crushed. Add the melted butter and pulse again until evenly mixed. Press half the mixture into the base of a 24 cm springform pan and the remaining half around the sides, making sure the crust is an even thickness. Refrigerate for at least 30 minutes while you make the filling.

3 Strain the strawberries in a sieve, reserving the liquid, then return the strawberries to the fridge. In a small saucepan over medium heat, reduce the liquid for about 5 minutes, taking care that it does not burn. Remove from the heat and measure out ½ cup of the liquid into a jug. Sprinkle the jelly crystals into the jug and mix with a fork to dissolve, then leave to cool.

4 Beat the cream cheese, egg yolks, caster sugar and vanilla together until smooth and creamy. Add the cooled jelly mixture and beat well. Pour into the crust and smooth evenly with a spatula. Chill in the fridge for at least 15 minutes. When the mixture has begun to set, arrange most of the strawberries on the top, reserving ½ cup to use to decorate the final layer. Return the cheesecake to the fridge to chill for 30 minutes.

5 Fold the passionfruit pulp through the whipped cream then spread over the layer of strawberries. Don't smooth the cream too much as it looks especially luscious when spread with abandon. Use the reserved strawberries to adorn the top and if you're feeling very courageous, add some white chocolate curls. Carefully remove the springform pan and serve.

Serves 10

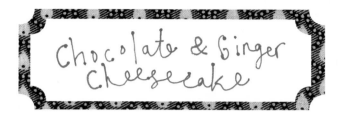

Chocolate & Ginger Cheesecake

This is a wickedly rich cheesecake that's not for the faint-hearted. Buderim glacé ginger has a dark exotic flavour that pairs perfectly with dark chocolate. This is the ultimate winter dessert served with a good Cognac or Grand Marnier. It can be made the night before you need it, as the flavours improve with time.

Method

1 To make the crust, crush the biscuits, hazelnuts and ground spices together in a food processor and add the melted butter. Process for 20 seconds, then press half the mixture into the base of a 24 cm springform pan and the other half around the sides, making sure the crust is an even thickness. Refrigerate for at least 30 minutes while you make the filling.

2 Using a double boiler or a heatproof bowl that fits snugly over a pan of boiling water, melt the chocolate chips until smooth and runny then take off the heat to cool slightly. In a mixing bowl, beat the cream cheese, sugar, ground ginger and 1 tablespoon of the liqueur (if using).

3 Add the gelatine and cocoa to the boiling water in a small cup. If the gelatine doesn't dissolve completely, sit the cup in boiling water and mix with a fork.

4 Add the egg yolks to the melted chocolate and mix until smooth, then add the chocolate mixture and the gelatine mixture to the cream-cheese mixture, and beat until all the ingredients are well combined. Chill in the fridge for 10 minutes.

5 Fold the chopped ginger and the remaining tablespoon of liqueur (if using) into the whipped cream, then fold this into the cream-cheese mixture and pour into the crust. Smooth the surface with a spatula or knife and chill until ready to serve.

Serves 10

Ingredients

Crust

1 × 400 g packet chocolate-chip cookies

140 g ginger snaps (the Swedish variety if you can find them)

1 cup ground roasted hazelnuts

pinch ground cloves

pinch ground ginger

130 g melted butter

Filling

1 cup chocolate chips

500 g cream cheese

½ cup caster sugar

pinch ground ginger

2 tablespoons Licor 43 liqueur or Grand Marnier (optional)

1 × 10 g sachet powdered gelatine

⅓ cup cocoa powder

⅓ cup boiling water

2 egg yolks, lightly beaten

125 g Buderim glacé ginger, finely chopped

300 ml thickened cream, whipped

FIESTA

DIPS

Dips are such an easy way to get a dinner party swinging as they can be made in advance and devoured while you're serving the cocktails. I always make extra as my children will happily gobble them up anytime. Be adventurous with the vegetables you serve your dips with: carrots and celery are standard, but witlof and baby radishes can give the platter a real zing.

Beetroot Dip

Makes about 2 cups

Beetroot really reaches its full potential after a couple of hours in a slow oven. I am happy to eat beetroot raw, boiled or even juiced, but once you've slow-roasted this handsome vegetable, there's no going back.

Ingredients

1 cup roasted ground cashew nuts
1 bunch beetroot, leaves and stalks trimmed (about 2 cm stalk retained), well washed, beets cut in half
¾–1 cup olive oil, plus extra for brushing
sea salt and freshly ground black pepper
1 cup freshly grated parmesan cheese
juice of 1 lemon
1 teaspoon hot chilli sauce

Method

1 Preheat the oven to 170˚C and line a large baking tray with foil.

2 Roast the cashew nuts by placing them on a plate in the microwave. Cook on the highest setting for 1 minute, them remove them and give the plate a shake to redistribute them. Cook on the highest setting for a further minute or until they turn golden, then set aside to cool.

3 With a pastry brush, paint the beetroot halves all over with olive oil then lay them flat on the tray. Season well and roast for 2–2½ hours until tender, turning and basting them with more olive oil and seasoning every 30 minutes.

4 Roughly chop the beetroot, place in a food processor with the cashew nuts, cheese, lemon juice and hot chilli sauce and mix for about 30 seconds. With the motor running, gradually add the olive oil in a thin, steady stream until you reach your desired consistency, then taste for seasoning and serve.

Hummus

Makes at least 2 cups

When I first met my future husband Simon, he was living in a bachelor pad, and the adorable lady who ran his local fruit shop would lovingly stash a tub of hummus in with his lonely bananas. I don't know if she was flirting with him or just being motherly, but I didn't care – the hummus was to-die-for. I soon started experimenting making my own, and this is the result. Now I find myself packing little parcels of hummus and crackers for my loved ones, just like the lady in the fruit shop – maybe there's a secret hummus club?

Ingredients

3 × 400 g cans chickpeas, 2 cans drained
1 tablespoon sesame oil
juice of 1 lemon
4 cloves garlic, crushed
pinch cayenne pepper, plus extra to garnish
pinch ground cumin
⅓ cup olive oil
sea salt and freshly ground black pepper
seeds from ½ a pomegranate, to garnish (optional)

Method

1 Place the drained chickpeas in a blender and purée until smooth. Add the remaining can of chickpeas with the water from the can, and the rest of the ingredients, puréeing to a thick paste. Taste for seasoning and add more of whatever you feel it needs.

2 If the hummus is too thick, blend in a little more lemon juice to thin it out. Transfer to a serving bowl, drizzle over some olive or sesame oil and sprinkle with some extra cayenne pepper. Scatter the pomegranate seeds on top, if using, for a sweet, crunchy finish.

Cio & Geoff's Dip

Makes about 1 cup

My sister Cio and her husband Geoff have played a huge role in Lil's life – they are like a great big security blanket for her. As far as family goes, it doesn't get any better than them. Games day at their place is a regular gathering of the cousins, where everyone brings something wicked to eat and we play endless hilarious rounds of charades, Pictionary and Trivial Pursuit. This dip is always on the menu, served with crackers and a good charade.

Try to find young ginger for this, as the older, gnarlier ginger tends to be much hotter and not as sweet.

Ingredients

4 × 5 cm knobs ginger, peeled and finely chopped
½ bunch spring onions, trimmed and finely chopped
⅓ cup peanut or canola oil
1 scant teaspoon sea salt

Method

1 Place all the ingredients in a blender and purée to a thick paste.

2 Transfer the paste to a heavy-based frying pan or wok and fry for a couple of minutes over medium heat. When the mixture becomes aromatic, remove from the heat and leave to cool to room temperature. Serve with sesame or lavash crackers.

Pork, Chicken & Coriander
Meatballs

It's always good to have a few dishes up your sleeve that are more or less foolproof. These make wonderful nibbles to serve with drinks, or can be made into a light meal with some ginger and spring-onion dip and steamed rice. Another alternative is to stuff the mixture into large red capsicums and bake, covered with foil, in an 180°C oven for 45 minutes.

If you have the time, let the meatball mixture sit for a while to allow the flavours to intensify; this step is not essential but will make the end result even yummier.

Ingredients

½ cup pine nuts

1 × 8 cm knob ginger, finely chopped

3 cloves garlic, finely chopped over 1 teaspoon salt to make a paste

1 red onion, very finely chopped

1–2 small chillies, deseeded and finely chopped

¼ cup chopped coriander leaves

½ cup water chestnuts, chopped

600 g pork mince

500 g chicken mince

2 eggs, lightly whisked

sea salt and freshly ground black pepper

⅓ cup plain flour

vegetable or canola oil, for frying

½ bunch coriander, leaves chopped

Cio and Geoff's Dip (see page 69), to serve

Method

1 Roast the pine nuts by placing them on a plate in the microwave and cooking on the highest setting for 1 minute. Remove them and give the plate a shake to redistribute them. Cook on the highest setting for a further minute or until they turn golden, then set aside to cool.

2 Place the ginger, garlic, onion, chilli, coriander, water chestnuts and roasted pine nuts in a large bowl and mix together. Add the pork and chicken mince, the eggs and some salt and pepper and, using your fingers, knead all the ingredients together, really squishing the mixture so everything gets well distributed. If you're not going to fry these straight away, cover the bowl with plastic film and refrigerate until ready.

3 When ready to cook, take about a tablespoonful of mixture and roll it into a small ball, then roll in the flour to coat completely. Pass the meatball from hand to hand to shake off any excess flour, set aside on a plate, then repeat until all the mixture is used.

4 Have a plate with a few sheets of paper towel on it ready for the cooked meatballs. Heat some oil over high heat in a medium-sized heavy-based frying pan. When the oil is hot, reduce the heat a little and drop in about eight meatballs (be careful not to crowd the pan) – they should sizzle immediately. Cook for about 30 seconds on each side until golden all over, then transfer to the plate to drain and continue with the next batch.

5 Serve the cooked meatballs on a large platter garnished with chopped coriander, alongside a bowl of dip and some toothpicks to help guests dunk their meatballs.

Makes about 45 small meatballs

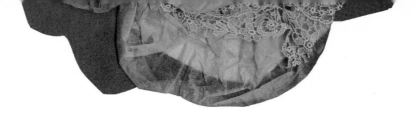

San Choi Bao

I first tried san choi bao at the old Tai Pei restaurant in Sydney; I was three years old. In the late sixties, this restaurant was the pinnacle of Chinese cuisine and whenever my father had to entertain his advertising clients, he'd take us there. The place was packed to the rafters with Chinese families laughing, arguing and eating. Large plates with hand-picked, writhing morsels from the fish tank were marched past, soon to be cooked and dressed in ginger and spring onions and presented with a flourish.

Often all the hustle and bustle meant a bit of a wait for our food, and that's when I would escape from the table and go exploring. I discovered that by standing and looking forlornly at other people's meals, I would attract a handful of exotic titbits and sometimes, to my mother's horror, I'd even sit down at other families' tables and eat with them, which is how I had my first taste of san choi bao. Years later, for Lil's birthday we created a huge Oriental banquet with numerous courses, and the san choi bao made its debut for the next generation.

Method

1 Heat 2 tablespoons of the oil in a wok or large frying pan. Add half the garlic, a tablespoon of the ginger, the chopped chilli, the pork and chicken mince and stir-fry until the mince is cooked through and just beginning to brown. Remove from the pan and set aside.

2 Wipe out the pan, heat the remaining oil then add the water chestnuts, the spring onions and the rest of the garlic and ginger. Stir-fry for about 2 minutes, then add the chopped coriander and the mince mixture and season. Stir-fry to combine all the ingredients for a minute or two – the mince should be just a little crunchy and caramelised.

3 Serve the mince filling on a large platter accompanied by the lettuce cups. A good hostess will first serve a lettuce cup and then gracefully add the filling. Have finger bowls at the ready as this can be a messy one to eat!

Serves 6

Ingredients

⅓ cup peanut oil

4 cloves garlic, crushed

2 × 8 cm knobs ginger, finely chopped (about ⅓ cup)

2 fresh chillies, deseeded and finely chopped

600 g pork mince

600 g chicken mince

½ cup sliced water chestnuts

6 spring onions, finely chopped

½ bunch chopped coriander

sea salt and freshly ground black pepper

8–10 iceberg lettuce leaves, washed and trimmed into baskets

Devils on Horseback

I have been making these hors d'oeuvres for years but I'm sure they were originally a great fifties innovation, probably served with a good martini. I have always thought they make perfect party starters as the sweet and savoury combination goes so well with a variety of drinks.

Ingredients

24 large pitted prunes
1 × 300 g block cream cheese, chilled,
　cut into 2 cm × 1 cm chunks
12 rashers rindless streaky bacon,
　cut in half lengthways

Method

1 Preheat the oven to 180°C, line a large baking tray with foil and smear on a little butter.

2 Stuff the prunes with a chunk of cream cheese, then wrap each one in a piece of bacon, securing with a toothpick where the bacon overlaps. Place on the baking tray and cook for 20 minutes until the bacon is slightly golden and just crispy (although the cooking time here is a matter of personal taste; if you like it crispier leave it in for a few minutes more). Serve on cheeky cocktail serviettes with your favourite beverage.

Makes 24

Devil's Delight

These are a wicked alternative to Devils on Horseback (see left). I was inspired to create these little delicacies when my fig tree produced the sweetest little purple figs – I thought they would be a good alternative to the prunes.

Ingredients

1 cup sweet sherry
24 small fresh figs, base cut with an 'x' shape
300 g hard blue cheese or taleggio, cut into
　2 cm × 1 cm chunks
12 thin slices prosciutto, *jamón serrano*
　or pancetta
red chillies, cut in half or left whole, to garnish

Method

1 Preheat the oven to 180°C, line a large baking tray with foil and smear on a little butter. Pour the sherry into a shallow dish and sit the figs in the liquid for about 15 minutes.

2 Remove the figs from the dish and stuff each one with a chunk of cheese, then wrap in a piece of cured meat, securing with a toothpick where the meat overlaps. Bake for 10–15 minutes, then serve garnished with a few red chillies to complete the devilish theme.

Makes 24

Chicken Drumettes

As a child, my brother Ignatius was a keen cook. He was never intimidated in the kitchen – he would try anything. Long before Asian food was popular in Australia, he was experimenting with the eclectic contents of our mother's pantry and creating delectable treats straight out of Chinatown.

Our mother worked full time and attended university most nights, studying for a degree in Anthropology, which gave Ignatius free rein in the kitchen. I remember many nights sitting at the kitchen counter, watching him baste chicken or pork ribs as they spluttered under a hot grill. This recipe of his was always a hit. I use drumettes as they are easy for guests to eat at parties and they look delightful generously stacked on a serving platter, but you can use any cut of chicken – just adjust the cooking time accordingly.

Method

1 Start a day or two before you want to serve these. In a large, heavy-based saucepan, melt the butter with the olive oil over low heat. Add the garlic and honey and stir until well combined and syrupy.

2 Remove the pan from the heat, add all the remaining ingredients except the chicken drumettes and coriander and mix well.

3 Place the drumettes in a stainless-steel bowl or plastic container and pour over the marinade, distributing it evenly over the chicken with a pastry brush. Refrigerate overnight or for 1–2 days to let the flavours develop.

4 When you're ready to cook these, preheat the grill to medium and cover a baking tray with foil. Working in batches, lay the drumettes out in rows, just touching each other. Brush a little of the marinade over them, then place under the grill until the chicken is golden.

5 Turn the drumettes over with a pair of tongs and lightly brush with some more marinade. Return them to the grill and cook until the chicken is dark brown and cooked through. Repeat with the remaining drumettes, then serve on a platter garnished with fresh coriander.

Serves a crowd

Ingredients

125 g butter

½ cup olive oil

10 cloves garlic, finely chopped with 1 teaspoon salt to make a paste

1 cup honey

3 red chillies, finely chopped

2 cups light soy sauce

3 × 8 cm knobs ginger, finely chopped (about ½ cup)

¼ cup hoisin sauce

1 teaspoon freshly ground black pepper

¼ teaspoon ground coriander

½ teaspoon five-spice powder

2 kg chicken drumettes

freshly chopped coriander, to garnish

SANGRIA

Lemonade

Sherry

here is nothing worse than bad sangria, and I must admit that I've persevered with quite a few, hoping they'd improve by the time I got to the bottom of the jug. Don't be mistaken and think that sangria is just a punch made from leftover cheap wines and fruit salad consumed at an Ibizan dance rave. If you have a lot of different alcohols and wines and you want to make a punch, then go crazy but don't call it sangria. Believe it or not, there is a standard recipe and, although certain quantities of ingredients may vary, if you stick to the basics outlined here, you can't go wrong.

Spain in summer is unbelievably hot and a jug of sangria is the perfect thirst-quencher. Floating apples and oranges on top gives it a unique flavour and also helps to soak up some of the alcohol.

I always make a huge batch of this. If you have leftovers at the end of the night, pour them into a plastic container and freeze – they will make a heavenly granita shaved into a glass for another time. Once you've mastered good sangria, master the traditional toast: *salut, amor y pesetas* (health, love and wealth).

Method

1 In a large stockpot, heat the sugar with the sherry, brandy and cinnamon stick over medium heat, stirring constantly and being careful not to let the mixture boil. As soon as the sugar has dissolved and the mixture is syrupy, remove the stockpot from the heat and leave to cool to room temperature before chilling (this mixture is called the *madre*, which means the mother).

2 Slice the oranges and core and dice the apples, then add the fruit to the cooled *madre* to prevent the apples browning.

3 Pour the chilled *madre* and fruit into a large punchbowl, and add the red wine, lemonade and Fanta. Give it a good stir, taste to see if it needs any adjustments, and serve, ladelling some fruit into each glass.

Makes about 8 litres (enough for a big party)

Ingredients

1 cup sugar

1 litre medium–dry sherry

1 litre brandy (does not have to be top-shelf quality)

1 stick cinnamon

1 bag oranges

1 bag apples

4 litres red wine (a good cask wine is perfect)

2 × 1-litre bottles lemonade

2 × 1-litre bottles Fanta (or equivalent)

Salut, amor y pesetas
(Health, love and wealth)

SPANISH HARLEM
A CELEBRATION OF PAELLA

Growing up in a Spanish/Filipino/American household in Sydney with fun-loving but somewhat eccentric parents has to be a large contributing factor to my love of a good party, and the food that inevitably goes with it.

When I was four years old, my parents decided to bring Spain to Wahroonga by celebrating the festival of San Fermin, a riotous event held each year in Pamplona that not only includes the consumption of huge amounts of red wine, but also acres of paella and other Spanish delicacies. All this is accompanied by maniacal music performed by whoever is drunk enough, and the day culminates in the famous running of the bulls.

In preparation for our own version of this fiesta, my father Nestor spent a fortnight training my brothers and cousins in the complicated art of 'killing the bull' – in this case, the bull was the front wheel and handlebars of an old bicycle with a set of real bull horns attached to it, pushed around by my father draped in a black cape. My Grandma Mary, a fine couturier, created toreador outfits for the boys and flamenco dresses for the girls (mine was always known as my 'olé' dress). All the adults wore variations on the traditional costume of a white shirt, white pants, red neckerchief and beret. To get our neighbours and new-found Aussie friends into the spirit of things, Mum and Dad insisted that, in true Spanish style, everyone's garage be converted into a *bodega* (drinking hole) and that they should all master drinking from the *porron* (a glass decanter with a pointy spout) or the *bota* (a leather pouch).

After what can only be described as a suburban Spanish 'pub' crawl with everyone stopping off at various *bodegas* on the way, the crowd arrived at my parents' house, consumed more wine and tapas, then finally ate the paellas. This was followed by the bullfight, our backyard having been transformed into a *corrida* for the occasion. The toreadors paraded, while the young girls threw roses into the centre of the bullring. When the bull stumbled in, a little the worse for wear from the pub crawl, it took no time at all for the youngsters to dispose of him.

PAELLA À LA IGNATIUS

There has never been any fear of cooking in our family, and as a result we aren't scared to tackle even the most challenging recipes. My brother adapted this from my mother's original paella recipe, refining and simplifying it over the years so that it has now become a classic in its own right. It's best made in a paella pan, but if you don't have one you can use a wide, shallow thin-based pan instead. The secret is to make sure the rice is not overcooked, but has had time to stand and absorb all the wonderful flavours. This standing period is called *reposar* – the act of resting. A truly authentic paella also has a crunchy, almost-but-not-quite-burnt base, called a *socorat*, that is considered a delicacy.

It can be tricky to find calasparra, the authentic Spanish paella rice. It's a medium-grain, high-quality absorbent white rice and whenever I see it I always stock up. Look for it in specialist food shops.

Ingredients

1 kg small black mussels, trimmed and debearded

sea salt and freshly ground black pepper

1 bunch flat-leaf parsley, leaves finely chopped, a few sprigs reserved for garnish

4 bay leaves, optional

2 sprigs rosemary, optional

1 × 750 ml bottle dry white wine

2–3 scampi

6–8 cups chicken stock

olive oil, for cooking

½ kg chicken thighs, cut into bite-sized pieces

½ kg small chicken drumsticks

2 large pork chops, cut into bite-sized pieces

2 large onions, diced

6 cloves garlic, finely chopped

2 large chorizos, thinly sliced

2 large red capsicums or pimientos (Spanish peppers), white insides and seeds removed, diced

½ kg prawns (the larger, the better), peeled and deveined

½ kg calamari, cleaned and cut into rings

4 cups calasparra rice

4–6 strands saffron

1 teaspoon smoked paprika

2 tablespoons lemon juice

1 cup frozen peas

6 hard-boiled eggs, cut into wedges, to garnish

Method

1 Place the mussels in a stockpot or a large deep saucepan with a generous sprinkle of salt and pepper, half the chopped parsley and some bay leaves or rosemary, if using. Add 2 cups white wine (and pour a large glass for yourself if you feel you need it!). Cover, bring to a boil and steam for about 3 minutes, then add the scampi and steam for a further 2 minutes. Take the pan from the heat, remove the scampi and set aside. Strain the cooked mussels through a sieve, reserving the cooking liquid and discarding any unopened mussels. Open the mussel shells, snap off the empty half and discard. Voila . . . the mussels are ready! Set them aside while you prepare the other ingredients.

2 Heat the stock in a small saucepan until simmering. Meanwhile, put a generous splash of olive oil in a wide, shallow thin-based pan and, working in batches, brown the chicken, then the pork, adding more oil as required (be careful not to let the oil burn). Once golden brown, drain the meat on some paper towel and season with salt and pepper.

3 Using the same pan, fry the onions and garlic until the onions are translucent. Add the chorizos and fry for a couple of minutes (as they cook they release their juices and create an amazing flavour). Throw in the diced capsicum or pimientos and cook for about 5 minutes, until softened. Transfer the ingredients to a plate and reserve.

4 Toss the prawns and calamari into the pan and cook in the remaining oil for 1½ minutes, then remove with a slotted spoon and set aside. Add the rice to the pan and toss gently so each grain is lightly coated with oil. As it cooks, the rice will turn white – this is when I throw in the rest of the parsley, the saffron, the paprika and a sprinkle of salt and pepper. Add enough simmering stock to cover the rice, bring to a boil then simmer, uncovered, for 10 minutes.

5 Add the lemon juice, frozen peas and the chorizo mixture then arrange the chicken, pork, mussels, prawns and calamari on top – make sure the mussels are facing up and are well buried in the rice so they stay moist. Cook, uncovered, over low–medium heat for 20 minutes, then remove the pan from the heat. The rice should be cooked but still have a little bite. Arrange the scampi flamboyantly on top, cover with foil and leave to stand for 10 minutes.

6 To serve, garnish with some parsley sprigs and the hard-boiled eggs and proudly present your masterpiece. Congratulations, you're now part of the family.

Serves at least 12

HOUSEBOAT PIE

This is my daughter Lil's recipe and, like all the best ones, it has evolved over the years. The first time she made this was on a houseboat holiday in Myall Lakes with six friends. She had nominated herself to do the cooking (the crew nicknamed her Betty Crocker) and set about the unenviable task of organising dinner for six vegetarians for five nights. In the nick of time Lil remembered that her father Ian had a great recipe for spinach pie so, finding a pocket of mobile phone reception between two islands, she gave him a call and took down the recipe on the back of a map. Even though they only had two pots, one burner and a dodgy oven that the pie tray didn't fit into, she ended up making a delicious pie that went swimmingly with the copious amounts of red wine ingested. The girl she was wooing at the time (now her partner, the gorgeous Mon Chew) liked it so much that it became a staple for many future dinner parties.

This indulgent pie can no longer take its name from its original key ingredient: spinach. It has become a pie so crammed with vegetables and cheese that it has been re-christened Houseboat Pie after the first time Lil made it. This dish can be done on the cheap or you can use indulgent cheeses like bocconcini, good-quality parmesan and Bulgarian feta. Make extra as it's great for lunch the next day.

Method

1 Preheat the oven to 180°C.

2 Slice the spinach leaves lengthways along the stem and lay one piece on top of the other. Roll them up into a tube and slice thinly into strips.

3 In a large, heavy-based saucepan, heat the oil over medium heat and fry the onion until translucent. Throw in the asparagus and fry until vibrant green. Add the spinach and 1 cup wine and stir in. As the spinach begins to reduce, add another ½ cup wine and 1 cup stock. Continue to cook for another 5 minutes or so, until the spinach has softened and reduced to a mass of green. Remove from the heat and leave to cool, then drain off any excess liquid to ensure the mixture isn't too runny.

4 Meanwhile, boil the potatoes in plenty of salted water until just cooked (or cook in the microwave on high for 8 minutes or until soft). Let cool and then gently combine them with the spinach mixture.

5 Break the eggs into a large bowl and beat, adding a pinch of salt and plenty of black pepper. Add the cheeses and combine.

6 Line a large pie dish with puff pastry, ensuring that the entire base and sides are covered (the pastry can overlap as long as it is well sealed). Spoon the spinach and potato mixture into the dish and pour the cheesy sauce over the top, smoothing it with a spoon to ensure an even surface. Cover with another sheet of puff pastry and seal the sides over the edges of the dish, making sure there are no gaps. Cook for 1 hour or until the pastry is golden.

Serves 6

Ingredients

1 bunch English spinach, stalks trimmed, leaves well washed

olive oil, for cooking

1 brown onion, diced

1–2 bunches asparagus, cut in half

½ × 750 ml bottle dry white wine

1 litre vegetable stock

2 large potatoes, peeled and thinly sliced

6 eggs

sea salt and freshly ground black pepper

500 g grated tasty cheese

350 g bocconcini, sliced

200 g feta, crumbled

150 g grated parmesan, optional

6 sheets frozen puff pastry, thawed

Chocolate Mousse

It was Oscar Wilde who said, 'The only way to resist temptation is to yield to it.' When it comes to chocolate mousse, I'm with Oscar; I find it very hard to resist, although I am happy with just a taste, as I am still searching for the ultimate mousse experience. I see it as my life's quest.

When Lil turned twenty I asked her what she would like me to make – her answer was 'the killer chocolate mousse', a Stephanie Alexander recipe that was a family favourite. As this seemed like a good occasion to pull out all the stops, I got hold of an enormous martini glass and we set out to create the ultimate chocolate mousse extravaganza, using Stephanie's recipe as a guide. I layered milk-chocolate and orange-chocolate mousse with the bittersweet chocolate, and that martini glass of madness ended up feeding about 25 people – it was quite a memorable dish. This is a toned-down version of that one, again based on Stephanie's recipe but with a few tweaks that I've made over the years.

Ingredients

250 g bittersweet chocolate, broken into small pieces
125 g unsalted butter
4 eggs, separated
1 teaspoon vanilla extract
½ cup caster sugar
300 ml thickened cream

Method

1 Melt the chocolate using a double boiler or in a heatproof bowl that fits snugly over a saucepan of boiling water. Add the butter and mix through the chocolate until smooth, then remove from the heat and transfer to a mixing bowl.

2 Whisk the egg yolks with a fork, then pour a small amount into the chocolate mixture and combine with a wooden spoon. Repeat until all the egg yolk is combined. Add the vanilla and mix well, then set aside.

3 Whisk the eggwhites until stiff, then gradually add the caster sugar, whisking between additions, until stiff peaks form. Gently fold this into the chocolate mixture with a whisk. Transfer to the fridge to chill.

4 Whip the cream and gently fold into the chilled chocolate mixture, then chill for another hour. Transfer to individual glasses and serve.

Serves 6

I 've learnt so much from my Grandma Mary, who has lived through many ups and downs in her 101 years. The most important thing she has passed onto me, though, is a passion for food. Every meal she makes is an offering of love, and she always uses the best possible ingredients. She would take particular care with her Christmas cake, baking it in November and continually dousing it with alcohol right up until Christmas Day.

When our large family gets together at Christmas, in the midst of the chaos and activity I so look forward to the foil-wrapped brick of cake hiding under the tree with one of Mary's unmistakeable handwritten cards. It's hard to believe that at her age she still has the energy to make a fruitcake for all her grandchildren.

Method

1 Preheat the oven to 160°C and line a deep 18 cm diameter cake tin with two layers of brown paper and a layer of greaseproof paper.

2 Place the nuts and chopped fruit in a large mixing bowl. Sift the flour and baking powder into the bowl, add the sugar and stir to combine.

3 Whisk the eggs until thick and fluffy. Add the vanilla to the eggs, then pour this over the fruit mixture. Combine all the ingredients to a thick dough, then spread the mixture evenly in the lined cake tin.

4 Place the tin on the middle shelf of the oven and bake for 2 hours. Test to see if the cake is ready by inserting a skewer into the middle of the cake; if it comes out clean, then remove the cake from the oven; if not, continue cooking until ready.

5 Cool in the tin on a wire rack. Once completely cool, wrap in foil, place in an airtight container and store in a cool, dark place. Every few days until you're ready to eat the cake, give it a little bit of Christmas cheer by spooning over some white rum or brandy to keep it moist.

6 Slice into very thin pieces to serve.

Serves 12

Ingredients

375 g shelled
brazil nuts

125 g pecans or walnuts

125 g glacé peaches,
finely chopped

125 g glacé apricots,
finely chopped

125 g glacé pineapple,
finely chopped

125 g glacé cherries,
finely chopped

125 g pitted dates,
finely chopped

90 g plain flour

2 teaspoons
baking powder

185 g caster sugar

3 large eggs

1 tablespoon
vanilla extract

1 litre white rum
or brandy

Triple Trouble Trifle

Trifle is such an English dessert, and with our Spanish roots it was not one we came across very often. The Spanish make a wickedly rich, alcohol-drenched, custard-based dish called *natillas*, but it's not really a trifle.

When I first started seeing my future husband Simon, in an effort to impress both him and his friends I threw him a birthday party in which the food (all nine courses) was either black or hot pink. It was my way of celebrating the union of two such disparate souls – black for his dark, mysterious nature and pink for my enthusiastic, eclectic personality. This was the dessert I made: a pink-and-black layered trifle.

This is one hell of a trifle and the beauty of it is that it improves overnight, so you can make it at least a day in advance. I always feel good if my dessert is well and truly out of the way when preparing for a big celebration or dinner party, as it means I can concentrate on being the host.

A word of warning: do not drive home after consuming a piece of this!

Ingredients

2 punnets fresh strawberries, hulled and sliced into quarters lengthways

2 cups caster sugar

1 cup Cointreau

½ cup freshly squeezed orange juice, strained

2 punnets fresh raspberries

1 cup framboise or other raspberry liqueur

600 g fresh or frozen blackberries *or* fresh pitted black cherries

1 cup Kirsch

900 ml thickened cream

1 teaspoon vanilla extract

2 round sponge or pound cakes, cut in half lengthways

2 jam swiss rolls, cut into 10 mm rounds

fresh berries and icing sugar, to garnish

Custard

4 egg yolks

2 tablespoons caster sugar

2 tablespoons cornflour

1 teaspoon vanilla extract

600 ml milk

1 teaspoon finely grated orange zest

Serves at least 12

Method

1 Place the strawberries in a bowl with ½ cup of the caster sugar, the Cointreau and the orange juice. Place the raspberries in another bowl with ½ cup of the caster sugar and the raspberry liqueur. Place the blackberries or cherries in another bowl with ½ cup of the caster sugar and the kirsch. Cover each bowl and chill in the fridge for at least 6 hours or overnight.

2 To make the custard, whisk the egg yolks in a small mixing bowl until just frothy. Add the sugar, cornflour, vanilla and ¼ cup milk, and whisk until smooth.

3 Heat the remaining milk in a double boiler or a heavy-based saucepan until very hot but not boiling. Take about ½ cup of the hot milk and add it to the egg mixture, whisking until well combined (this helps to cook the egg gradually and reduces the chance of the ingredients curdling). Add all the egg mixture to the hot milk in the pan and gradually bring to a boil, stirring constantly. Add the orange zest and keep stirring. The custard should be getting thick – when it's thick enough to coat the back of a spoon, it's ready. Remove from the heat and allow the custard to cool, covered closely with plastic film (this will prevent a thick skin forming).

4 Whip the cream with the remaining ½ cup of caster sugar and the vanilla.

5 Take a large glass bowl and place one round sponge half in the bottom. Line the sides of the bowl with the swiss roll rounds all the way up to the top, using them all and pressing them together so there are no gaps.

6 Arrange a layer of strawberries over the sponge and drizzle the syrup over the sides and base. Pour a thick layer of custard over the strawberries, then spoon a thin layer of whipped cream on top.

7 Place on another round sponge half and, with a skewer, make some holes in it so the syrup soaks through. Cover with half the blackberries or cherries and half their syrup. Pour over a thick layer of custard, then a thin layer of whipped cream and top with another sponge half, again pricking holes in it to allow the syrup to soak through.

8 Spoon over the raspberries and their syrup and spread out over the sponge. Add a layer of whipped cream then top with the final sponge half. Cover the whole thing with plastic film and place a large dinner plate on top, pushing gently to compact the layers.

9 Uncover and prick some holes in the top layer of sponge. Cover with the remaining blackberries or cherries and a final layer of custard. Spread whipped cream over the top and decorate with a few fresh berries and a sprinkling of icing sugar.

COMFORT
FOOD

There is nothing more satisfying than homemade soup.
Whenever I've wanted to let a person know that
I really love and care for them, I make them soup.
It fortifies the soul and seeps into
every nook and cranny of the body,
rejuvenating, nourishing and energising with love.

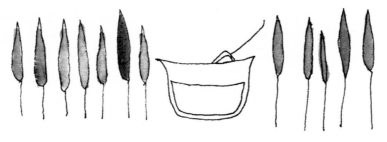

White Winter Soup

This is a great soup to make on those days when it rains solidly and even a trip to the shops seems too treacherous, as it can be made with whatever vegetables you have in the cupboard. Atticus and Oliver love days like this: they gather their doonas, blankets and stuffed toys and build a Noah's Ark, while I try out new recipes and produce home-baked delights for their approval. We've always called these doona days, and they're perfect for soup.

Method

1 In a large stockpot with a lid, melt the butter with the olive oil over low heat. Add the onion or leek and cook for about 10 minutes to caramelise. Add the parsnips, garlic and sugar, season with salt and pepper and cook for 5 minutes or so.

2 Add the chopped celery and just enough stock to cover the veggies, then increase the heat to high and bring to a boil. Reduce to a simmer and cook for 5 minutes, then add the potatoes and simmer for 10 minutes.

3 Add the cauliflower, the remaining stock and the marjoram, partially cover the pot with the lid and simmer over low heat for 2 hours.

4 Season to taste, then lightly mash with a potato masher to give it a soupy yet thick and chunky texture. Serve in individual bowls with a big dollop of sour cream and a sprinkling of marjoram.

Ingredients

25 g butter

2 tablespoons light olive oil

2 large white onions *or* washed and trimmed leeks, finely chopped

3 large parsnips, peeled and finely diced

2 cloves garlic, crushed

generous pinch sugar

sea salt and freshly ground black pepper

3 sticks celery, chopped

4 cups chicken, vegetable or beef stock

2 large potatoes, chopped into small cubes

½ cauliflower, chopped into small florets

2 tablespoons fresh marjoram, plus extra to serve

sour cream, to serve

Serves 6

Mon Chew's Chicken & Corn Soup

Lovely Mon Chew is Lil's girlfriend, and we consider her and her charming family very much part of our clan. Treasured recipes are passed down from mother to daughter in the Chew family, just as they are in ours.

This satisfying soup should really be called Chun Chew's chicken and corn soup, as it is Mon's mother, Chun's, recipe, but after a few years of house sharing, Mon has adapted this to suit a restricted budget! I am particularly fond of this soup, as it is low in fat and high in protein, and is always lovingly prepared for me by Lil or Mon.

Ingredients

4 chicken thigh fillets, trimmed of fat and chopped into small pieces
about 2 cups boiling water (enough to cover the chicken)
1 × 400 g can creamed corn
sea salt and freshly ground black pepper
1 egg
½ × 400 g can corn kernels
½ bunch spring onions, finely chopped

Method

1 Place the chopped chicken in a medium-sized saucepan and pour over enough boiling water to cover. Heat over high heat and cook, stirring, for about 5 minutes or until the chicken is cooked through.

2 Reduce the heat to medium, add the creamed corn and simmer, stirring, for 5 minutes. Season with salt and a generous slug of pepper then crack the egg into the soup, stirring constantly to distribute the egg evenly through the soup as it cooks.

3 Once the egg has been stirred in, reduce the heat to low and add the corn kernels to warm through. Garnish with finely chopped spring onions and serve.

Serves 4

chicken Soup for the Soul ...

When you're suffering from flu or a cold and feel too horrid to prepare anything for yourself, the greatest act of love is for someone to make you chicken soup. It was my brother Ignatius who let me in on the secret to a really strong, fortifying broth that will knock the socks off any ailment: cook the chicken in chicken stock – it makes it velvety, soft and especially soothing.

Try not to overcook the chicken as there's nothing worse than a tough old bird. The flesh of perfectly poached chicken will be a little pink but the juices should still run clear. Any leftovers can be refrigerated then reheated the next day as this soup improves with age.

Method

1 Heat some oil in a large stockpot, add the onion and celery and cook for 5 minutes. Throw in the carrots and cook for a further 5 minutes.

2 Add the ginger, garlic, chilli, peppercorns, coriander roots and stems, the whole chicken and the chicken stock. Simmer over low heat for 50 minutes, occasionally skimming any scum from the surface with a spoon. Check the chicken is cooked by piercing the thickest part of the leg with a skewer – if the juices are still bloody, continue simmering until cooked through.

3 Transfer the chicken to a cutting board and strip off the flesh, discarding the skin. Place in soup bowls with some coriander leaves, bean sprouts and chopped chilli, then ladle over the soup and serve.

Serves 6

Ingredients

olive oil, for cooking

2 large brown onions, roughly chopped

½ stick celery, chopped

4 carrots, chopped

1 × 8 cm knob ginger, roughly chopped

6 cloves garlic, chopped

2–3 red chillies, finely chopped

handful black peppercorns

1 bunch coriander, roots and 2.5 cm of the stems finely chopped, leaves picked

1 × 1.6 kg chicken

6–8 cups chicken stock (or enough to cover the chook)

bean sprouts, to serve

freshly chopped chilli, to garnish

The greatest act of love is
for someone to make you chicken soup.

SLOW-ROASTED ROOT VEGETABLES

All the tuber and root vegetables, such as potatoes, sweet potatoes, parsnips, beetroot, carrots, Jerusalem artichokes, yams and even radishes, are good to slow-roast. I love this method of cooking as it releases the natural sugars and enhances the earthy flavour of these underground dwellers. It's a marvellous way to cook – no fuss and the minimum of preparation for maximum results. I always scatter some fresh herbs over the veggies before roasting them: rosemary goes with just about everything; bay leaves increase that earthy flavour; marjoram adds a sweetness; and thyme, oregano and sage give a more Italian flavour with their assertive nature (don't overdo it with these).

If I have to do a lot of preparation for a dinner party, I slow-roast veggies the night before so they have time to cool before being added to salads and dips – this way they won't melt the other ingredients or make the salad leaves wilt! I usually scatter some garlic cloves amongst the roasting veggies as the resulting garlic purée is sweeter and less pungent than raw garlic, and it's so handy to have some ready when you need it. Simply squeeze the puréed pulp from the skin into a lidded jar and cover with a little olive oil. To make the garlic really sweet and mushy, drop the separated cloves into boiling water for 5 minutes before adding them to the roasting tin.

Ingredients

your choice of tuber or root vegetables, peeled and cut into similar-sized pieces
olive oil, for brushing
sea salt and freshly ground black pepper
chopped fresh herbs, for scattering
1–2 heads garlic, cloves separated but not peeled

Method

1 Preheat the oven to 150°C and line a baking tray with foil.

2 Scatter the veggies on the tray and brush with a light coating of olive oil. Season with salt and pepper and sprinkle with fresh herbs. Because the garlic takes less time to cook, I usually add it after the veggies have been cooking for about an hour.

3 Place the baking tray on the middle shelf of the oven so the heat will circulate evenly and bake for 30 minutes. Turn the veggies over, brush with more oil and season with salt and pepper. Return to the oven, cooking for 1–3 hours in total (depending on how crispy you like your veggies), turning them and brushing with oil every 30 minutes or so.

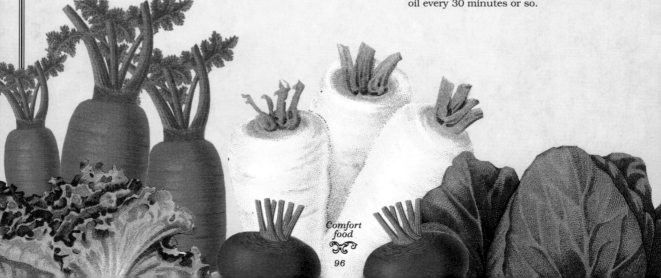

ROASTED ROMA TOMATOES

My love affair with Italy started the day a great big tomato was placed in front of me, bathed in oil and dressed with freshly ground black pepper, sea salt and basil. It was the middle of a very hot summer and this tomato looked like it was about to burst with all the sunshine it had absorbed. I will never forget it. For some reason tomatoes just taste better in Italy – perhaps it's because you're more likely to be eating them shortly after they've been picked. My mother is always bringing me baskets of fresh goodies from her farm, including tomatoes, so I am completely spoilt.

These roasted romas could not be simpler to prepare and can be served with so many things. They complement fish, chicken and mushrooms, and are fabulous with scrambled eggs and bacon. Sometimes I add some good-quality goat's cheese and a handful of fresh basil to the tomatoes for the last 30 minutes of cooking.

Ingredients

12 roma tomatoes,
 halved lengthways
caster sugar, for sprinkling
sea salt and freshly ground
 black pepper
olive oil, for cooking
2 large sprigs rosemary,
 brushed with olive oil

Method

1 Preheat the oven to 110°C and line a baking tray with foil.

2 Place the tomato halves on the tray, cut-side up, and sprinkle with a little caster sugar, salt and pepper. Drizzle with olive oil, lay the rosemary sprigs on top and roast for 2 hours.

Black-eyed Beans With Bacon Hock

There is something about the cold weather that brings out the true Spaniard in me – when the temperature drops, I immediately stock up on dried beans of all descriptions as well as ham hocks, chorizo and beef bones. These ingredients can easily be transformed into hearty, warming dishes that will get you through the longest winter.

Ingredients

500 g dried black-eyed beans, soaked in a large bowl of water for 2 hours, then rinsed

4 bay leaves

olive oil, for cooking

4 brown onions, finely chopped

6 cloves garlic, finely chopped with 1 teaspoon salt to make a paste

2 fresh red chillies, finely chopped

2 large red capsicums, white insides and seeds removed, diced

2 chorizos, sliced

1 × 1 kg ham hock, rinsed

about 8 cups beef stock (or enough to cover the ingredients in the pot)

1 large sprig rosemary

sea salt and freshly ground black pepper

2 cups brown rice

extra virgin olive oil and sherry vinegar, for drizzling

½ bunch flat-leaf parsley, finely chopped

Method

1 Place the beans in a large heavy-based saucepan with 6 cups water and 2 bay leaves. Bring to a boil and simmer for 20 minutes, then drain, rinse and set aside.

2 Meanwhile, heat a generous splash of olive oil over medium heat in a large heavy-based pan and fry the onions for about 10 minutes until softened. Add the garlic paste and chilli, turn the heat to low and cook for 5 minutes, then add the diced capsicum and cook until the capsicum starts to soften. Add the chorizo and cook for 5 minutes.

3 Add the ham hock, beans, just enough stock to cover the ingredients, the rosemary sprig and remaining bay leaves and season. Cover and gently simmer over low–medium heat for 1½ hours, stirring every 30 minutes or so. Remove the lid, taste for seasoning, and simmer for 15–30 minutes uncovered.

4 Meanwhile, put the brown rice in a saucepan with a lid and cover with cold water. Swish the rice around in the water to rinse, and then slowly pour the water out (being careful not to lose any rice down the sink). Place your middle fingertip directly on the surface of the rice and fill with water up your finger's first joint. Bring to a boil, then turn the heat down to the lowest setting, cover and cook for 20 minutes. Leave covered until ready to serve.

5 Serve the beans on the rice, drizzling over some extra virgin olive oil and sherry vinegar and garnishing with parsley.

Serves 6

Mushrooms in Parsley, Garlic & Sherry

When I think of Spain, I think of mushrooms. In Madrid, it's common practice to have a glass of sherry at around 5 p.m., accompanied by a little plate of mushrooms, a slice or two of *jamón* and a piece of *manchego* cheese. After such a great start to the evening, it's no wonder the Madrileños enjoy such a good nightlife.

Serve these as tapas or as part of an antipasto plate. They also make a delicious accompaniment to chicken or scrambled eggs, or, my favourite: served with toast and a thick slice of well-cooked bacon.

Method

1 Melt the butter with the oil in a heavy-based saucepan over medium heat. Add the crushed garlic and chilli and toss for a few seconds, making sure they don't burn.

2 Throw in the mushrooms and coat evenly with the oil and garlic – they should start to sweat a little but still hold their shape. Add the parsley, sliced garlic, salt and pepper and toss for about a minute before adding the sherry. Bring to a rollicking simmer for about 3 minutes, then cover and turn off the heat.

3 Taste and adjust the seasoning if necessary, then let the mushrooms cool to room temperature before serving.

Serves 6 as an entrée

Ingredients

50 g butter

generous splash olive oil

6 cloves garlic, 4 crushed,
    2 finely sliced

1 red chilli, deseeded and
    finely chopped

600 g fresh small–medium
    mushrooms

1 cup chopped
    flat-leaf parsley

1 teaspoon sea salt

1 teaspoon freshly ground
    black pepper

2 cups Spanish sherry (or
    white wine, if you prefer)

Fresh Pea & Chorizo
Risotto

Fresh peas straight from the pod inspire me to make salads and
risottos. At Galuzzos, the marvellous fruiterer that I frequent,
the ladies behind the counter can shell peas faster than any machine,
and while they're shelling, they'll rattle off a recipe or two along with
a few tried-and-true culinary tips.

The key to a perfect risotto is good-quality stock, so it really is worth
making your own if possible (I add stock cubes to mine just to intensify
the chickeny flavour). You can store any leftover stock in the fridge for
a few days, or freeze it in ice-cube trays and store in separate plastic
bags for later use.

This is a meal in itself but could also be served with steamed
asparagus or green beans. Any leftovers are delicious the next day.

Ingredients

20 g butter
2 tablespoons olive oil
2 large onions, finely chopped
2 leeks, well washed and
    finely sliced (outer leaves
    and tops reserved for stock)
3 cloves garlic, finely chopped
3 chorizos, chopped
1 red capsicum, white insides and
    seeds removed, finely chopped
    (optional)
2 cups arborio rice
250 g fresh peas
1 cup white wine
1 cup finely chopped flat-leaf parsley
sea salt and freshly ground
    black pepper
1 cup finely grated parmesan cheese

Chicken stock

2 chicken carcasses (ask your
    butcher for these)
2 chicken stock cubes
6 carrots, roughly chopped
2 cloves garlic, roughly chopped
4 sticks celery, roughly chopped,
    leaves added
8 peppercorns
1 sprig rosemary
2 bay leaves
outer leaves and tops of 2 leeks

Method

1 To make the stock, place all the ingredients in a large saucepan and cover with 6–8 cups water. Bring to a boil, then reduce the heat to the lowest possible setting. Simmer for 2 hours, skimming any scum from the top now and then with a large spoon, then strain the stock into a clean saucepan and keep at a low simmer (it's important to use hot stock when making risotto).

2 Melt the butter with the olive oil in a large heavy-based saucepan over medium heat. Add the onion and leek and fry for at least 5 minutes or until softened, then add the garlic and cook for a further 5 minutes. Throw in the chorizo and capsicum, then reduce the heat a little, cover and cook for 5 minutes.

3 Pour the rice into the pan with the onion mixture and stir constantly until the rice is well-coated. Increase the heat to medium, ladle in 2 cups of stock and keep stirring. When the rice has absorbed all the liquid, add the peas and another cup of stock, stirring constantly for about 12 minutes. Pour in the wine and give it a really good stir, then leave to simmer for about 5 minutes.

4 Pour in some more stock and most of the parsley (reserving a spoonful for the garnish) and season with salt and pepper. Check the texture – if the risotto is slightly soupy with a little bite to the rice, it's perfect. If not, add a little more stock and cook for a few more minutes. It's important not to overcook it otherwise it will become very starchy and heavy. To serve, sprinkle the parmesan over and garnish with the remaining parsley.

Serves 4–6

Lemon, Asparagus & Parmesan Pasta

This is one of the simplest pastas you can make: light, refreshing and incredibly delicious. The addition of some smoked salmon at the very end would take it to another level and make it worthy of a dinner party, but I find it makes a perfect lunchtime pasta just as it is.

Ingredients

40 g butter

¼ cup olive oil

1 large leek or 2 small leeks, trimmed and well washed, sliced into ½ cm rounds

2 bunches asparagus, woody ends discarded, spears cut into 3 cm lengths

2 cloves garlic, crushed

finely grated zest and juice of 1 lemon

½ bunch flat-leaf parsley, finely chopped

sea salt and freshly ground black pepper

1 cup freshly grated parmesan cheese

500 g spaghetti, farfalle or fettuccine

Method

1 Melt the butter with a teaspoon of the olive oil in a heavy-based saucepan over very low heat and fry the leeks for about 30 minutes until they become soft and creamy (you may need to use a simmer mat to keep the temperature low enough to prevent them burning).

2 Add the asparagus and garlic to the pan, increase the heat to medium and cook for 5 minutes. Combine the remaining olive oil, the lemon zest and juice, the parsley and some salt and pepper in a large bowl.

3 Meanwhile, bring a large pan of water to a boil and throw in the pasta with a drizzle of olive oil. Cook until al dente, drain and toss through the lemon-juice mixture. Add the leek and asparagus mixture and stir in the grated parmesan. Taste for seasoning and serve immediately.

Serves 4

One-pot Pasta

I have been making this pasta for years and have passed the recipe on to many young friends. Lil has improved the original with the addition of a good-quality balsamic vinegar. I usually serve this cold, but served warm as below the bocconcini melts into a cheesy pool of goodness, making it real comfort food.

Method

1 Bring a large pan of water to a boil and throw in the pasta with a drizzle of olive oil. Cook until al dente, then drain.

2 Meanwhile, place ¼ cup olive oil into a large salad bowl and add the bocconcini, tomato, garlic and basil then season with salt and pepper.

3 Add the drained pasta to the salad bowl and mix the ingredients together. Add a generous splash of balsamic vinegar, if using, sprinkle the parmesan over and toss through again. Taste for seasoning then serve immediately.

Serves 4

Ingredients

500 g spirelli pasta

¼ cup olive oil

1 × 180 g tub bocconcini, drained and sliced

6 roma tomatoes, sliced

3 cloves garlic, crushed

1 bunch fresh basil, leaves picked and roughly torn

sea salt and freshly ground black pepper

splash of good-quality balsamic vinegar (optional)

1 cup freshly grated parmesan cheese

TUNA MORNAY

In year nine (or third form, as it was known in my day) I had a very perky and committed home-science teacher whose name, believe it or not, was Mrs Yields. It was her mission to train us in all matters household-related. Had it not been for Mrs Yields' tuna mornay au gratin, I would not know how to make a decent béchamel today.

I regularly make my own version of tuna mornay and my kids love it. One word of advice, use a good-quality tuna in oil rather than in spring water – the tuna stays moist and has a better flavour. I often think of Mrs Yields, with her meticulously applied lipstick, her perfectly ironed apron and a French roll that would give any drag queen a run for their money, and wonder what she's doing now... hopefully enjoying time with her grandchildren and passing on vital cooking tips to the next generation.

I have to confess something here: I always thought that tuna mornay was a combination of good béchamel, tuna and the onion mixture. But when I began researching this recipe I discovered that a true mornay must have cheese in the béchamel! If you do want to add cheese, stir about 100 g each of grated gruyère and parmesan into the hot béchamel until the cheese is melted.

Method

1 Heat the butter and a generous splash of olive oil in a heavy-based frying pan over medium heat. Add the onion and garlic paste then reduce the heat to low, cover and cook until onion is soft, stirring occasionally. Stir in the celery and cook for a further 5 minutes.

2 Meanwhile, put the brown rice in a saucepan with a lid and cover with cold water. Swish the rice around in the water to rinse and then slowly pour the water out (being careful not to lose any rice down the sink). Place your middle fingertip directly on the surface of the rice and fill with water up to your finger's first joint. Bring to a boil, then turn the heat down to the lowest setting, cover and cook for 20 minutes. Leave covered until ready to serve.

3 Add the tuna to the onion mixture and stir in about 2 cups of béchamel sauce (use more or less, depending on your personal preference). Cook over low heat for a couple of minutes to just warm through.

4 Serve the mornay on a bed of rice and garnish with chopped chives or parsley and pepper.

Serves 4–6

Ingredients

20 g butter

olive oil, for cooking

3 large onions, finely chopped

3 cloves garlic, finely chopped with 1 teaspoon salt to make a paste

4 large sticks celery, finely chopped

2 cups brown rice

2 × 425 g tins good-quality tuna in oil

about 2 cups Béchamel (see page 6)

finely chopped chives or flat-leaf parsley, to serve

freshly ground black pepper

Roast Chicken
with Chorizo, Prune & Fig Stuffing

I've never been fond of traditional chicken stuffing. I have a stomach of steel but find it difficult to digest the stodgy combination of stale dried herbs permeating swollen breadcrumbs. My friend Meredith is gluten-intolerant, which has given me the perfect opportunity to create a breadcrumb-free, moist, flavoursome stuffing that seems to be a hit among those with or without an aversion to bread.

Marjoram is my favourite herb to go with baked chicken, but parsley, sage and rosemary also work well (the last two are slightly stronger so adjust the amounts or use a combination of herbs). If the figs are completely dried, soak them in a small cup of fresh orange juice for a few hours before combining them with the other ingredients.

Ingredients

olive oil, for cooking

2 large brown onions, sliced into 1 cm rings

1 large organic chicken, rinsed and dried with paper towel

1 chorizo, sliced

sea salt and freshly ground black pepper

1 handful chopped herbs

steamed rice or potatoes, to serve (optional)

Stuffing

1 large red onion, diced

2 chorizos, sliced

200 g pitted prunes, chopped in half

200 g semi-dried figs, chopped into quarters

¼ cup chopped fresh herbs

5 spring onions, finely chopped

4 cloves garlic, finely sliced

finely grated zest and juice of 1 orange

½ cup pine nuts or cashews (optional)

sea salt and freshly ground black pepper

pinch smoked paprika

small splash olive oil

you know who!

chorizo

prunes

figs

Method

1 Preheat the oven to 200°C and add a splash of olive oil to a heavy-based casserole or baking dish with a lid. Add the brown onion and toss in the oil until evenly coated.

2 To prepare the stuffing, place all the ingredients in a bowl and mix with your hands until evenly combined.

3 Take the neck-end of the chicken and fill with stuffing, leaving a little room for expansion. Seal by pulling the skin over and under, tucking it between the wings. In the wider opening, place as much stuffing as possible, using your fingers to really fill the carcass. Squeeze any excess stuffing between the skin and the flesh, then seal by pushing the parson's nose inside the opening. Rub a little of the stuffing juices on the outside of the chicken and arrange the chorizo slices on top. Season the whole chook with salt and pepper and sprinkle some fresh herbs over.

4 Place the chicken on the bed of onions, breast-side down (the breast meat needs less cooking time and all the juices running down will keep the flesh moist). Cover with a lid and bake for 30 minutes. Carefully take the chicken out of the oven and baste thoroughly with the juices that have formed in the pan. Return to the oven to bake for another 20 minutes.

5 Turn the chicken breast-side up, baste again, add a little more salt and pepper and return to the oven for 10 minutes uncovered. The chicken should be golden on the outside and when pricked with a skewer in the thickest part of the leg, the juices should run clear. If the juices are still pink, cook the chook for a little longer.

6 When the chicken is cooked, leave to rest for at least 10 minutes while you take everything else to the table. Carve the chicken and scoop out the stuffing, and serve on a bed of rice or with steamed potatoes.

Serves 6

Come my little creatures,
I've made a lovely crumble...

Perfect Peaches

When the first peaches appear, announcing the coming of summer, I start planning all the wonderful dishes I can create. There are more culinary options than you might think: yes, peaches are often used in desserts and cocktails, but I'm also rather partial to peach chutney served with a hot beef curry or the tangy combination of chilli garlic prawns with fresh peaches and finely sliced spring onions.

Poaching peaches in a vanilla-infused syrup is probably the most simple and delicious way of capturing their sunny flavour. I always poach them with their skins on as it helps preserve their girlie blush. This dish comes close to perfection for me; nothing compares with that first spoonful of rose-coloured syrup or the scent of vanilla blended dreamily with a perfect poached peach.

Ingredients

1 cup caster sugar
1 vanilla bean
6 large white or
 yellow peaches
pouring cream or
 good-quality vanilla bean
 ice cream, to serve

Method

1 Place the sugar, 2 cups water and the vanilla bean in a saucepan large enough to hold the peaches in a single layer, and simmer until the sugar has dissolved. Gently place the peaches in the syrup, then cover and simmer over low heat for 20 minutes (ensuring that the heat stays low – use a simmer mat if you have one and check that the pan is not drying out as you cook).

2 After 20 minutes, turn the heat off and let the peaches cool completely in the syrup.

3 Remove the peaches with a slotted spoon and make a small slit in each with a sharp knife. Carefully remove both skin and stone, trying not to bruise the flesh or alter the shape of the peach. Place the peaches in individual serving bowls and spoon some of the syrup over the top. Serve with a drizzle of cream or a scoop of ice cream.

Serves 6

Comfort food

Loki's Pears

I was given this recipe by Lil's friend Loki one winter, and the thought of buttery pears in a chocolate fudge sauce made me go out and get the ingredients straight away. The ideal pears for this dish would be the brown beurre bosc variety, but if you can't find them, substitute with any ripe pears. This fudge sauce is completely decadent and can be served with stewed fruit, a pudding or even used to top a cake that needs moistening.

Method

1 Preheat the oven to 180°C and butter a baking dish.

2 Peel the pears but retain the stems. Cut each pear in half from the stem to the base and carefully remove the seeds and core. Lay the pears in the baking dish, cut-side up then place ½ teaspoon of butter in each pear half, sprinkle ½ teaspoon brown sugar over the butter and douse each pear with enough marsala to lightly coat the flesh. Sprinkle a little cinnamon over everything.

3 Bake for 30 minutes, then give the pears another slurp of marsala, sprinkle with the remaining brown sugar and return to the oven for another 20 minutes. Test for tenderness – if they can be easily pierced with a fork, they are ready.

4 Meanwhile, to make the sauce, melt the chocolate chips and cream in the microwave on the highest setting for 2 minutes. Stir well, then heat again for a few seconds until smooth and runny. Alternatively, place the chocolate and cream in a bowl that fits snugly over a saucepan of boiling water until the chocolate has melted and the mixture is smooth and runny.

5 Serve the pears with ice cream and drizzle some of the cooking syrup on top, then spoon over a generous amount of fudge sauce to finish.

Serves 6

Ingredients

6 ripe pears

30 g butter

1½ tablespoons brown sugar

about 2 cups marsala

ground cinnamon, for sprinkling

coffee or vanilla ice cream, to serve

Chocolate fudge sauce

1½ cups dark chocolate chips

1 cup reduced-fat thickened cream

Jungle Jaffa Cake

I love the combination of orange and dark chocolate and I want everyone to be able to enjoy it, so here's a recipe suitable for the gluten-intolerant, who often have to steer clear of cakes. I've included chocolate icing, but it's not essential – this cake is so rich and moist it can easily stand alone.

Ingredients

2 large navel oranges
1 cup dark
  chocolate chips
250 g ground almonds
⅔ cup caster sugar
1 teaspoon
  bicarbonate of soda
6 eggs

Chocolate icing

250 g dark chocolate,
  broken into pieces
200 ml
  thickened cream

Method

1 Put the whole oranges in a saucepan, cover with water and boil for at least 2 hours, making sure the pan doesn't boil dry (keep a boiled kettle handy for topping up).

2 Remove the oranges and let them cool, then transfer to a plate or chopping board and cut into cubes, skin and all, retaining the juices but discarding any pips.

3 Melt the chocolate chips in the microwave on the highest setting for 2 minutes. Stir well, then heat again for a few seconds until smooth and runny. Alternatively, place the chocolate chips in a bowl that fits snugly over a saucepan of boiling water until the chocolate has melted.

4 Preheat the oven to 180°C. Butter a deep 24 cm cake tin and line with baking paper. Place the orange cubes and juice, along with the remaining cake ingredients in a blender or food processor and mix until well combined, scraping down the sides with a spatula. Pour the batter into the cake tin and bake for 40–50 minutes, or until the cake springs back when touched in the middle. Cool in the tin for a few minutes then transfer to a wire rack to cool completely.

5 To make the chocolate icing, melt the chocolate with the cream in a bowl that fits snugly over a saucepan of boiling water. Stir until the mixture is glossy and spreadable. Spread over the cooled cake and serve.

Serves 10

Chocolate SAND CAKE

As a child, it was very hard to remove me from the beach. I was terrified of the waves, but I was in heaven at the shore's edge building sandcastles. My mother says I loved the sand so much that I'd eat it on Jatz crackers (much to her horror). It's understandable, then, that when I found this handwritten recipe in an old cookbook, my curiosity got the better of me and I had to make it straight away. True to its name, it has quite a dry, sandy consistency. I imagine if you used fresh coconut the texture would be different, but then you wouldn't be able to call it sand cake, which I think is charming.

Method

1 Preheat the oven to 180°C and butter and line 2 × 25 cm diameter cake tins.

2 Cream the butter and sugar together until thick and pale. Add the eggs one at a time, beating well after each addition. Sift in the cocoa and flour, then add the coconut and mix until combined. Add the vanilla and ½ cup water and mix thoroughly.

3 Divide the batter among the cake tins and bake for 30–45 minutes or until cooked (a skewer inserted in the centre should come out clean). Cool in the tins for a few minutes, then turn out onto wire racks and leave to cool completely.

4 Place one cake on a serving plate and top with cherry jam then whipped cream. Sandwich the other cake on top.

5 To make the chocolate icing, melt the chocolate chips in a bowl that fits snugly over a saucepan of boiling water. Add the cream and stir until smooth.

6 Pour the icing over the cake, letting it drip down the sides. Use a butter knife to smooth the icing evenly around the sides and on top. Decorate with cherries or shredded coconut if you like.

Serves 12

Ingredients

250 g butter

1½ cups caster sugar

4 eggs

½ cup cocoa powder

2¼ cups self-raising flour

½ cup desiccated coconut

1 tablespoon vanilla extract

1 cup cherry jam

300 ml cream, whipped

fresh cherries or lightly toasted shredded coconut, to decorate (optional)

Chocolate icing

250 g chocolate chips

1 cup pouring cream

Rhubarb, Pear & Raspberry Crumble

When the weather starts turning and the leaves from the liquidambar trees that line my street start to fall, I know autumn is really upon us. As much as I mourn the departure of summer, I adore the colours of autumn, and the fruit and veggies that begin to make an appearance. Figs are still around and they are incredibly sweet, but it's the rhubarb, pears and raspberries that keep teasing me, whispering 'crumble, crumble, make us into crumble...'.

While this dish is perfect for chilly autumn nights, it's also wonderful for breakfast the next day (served at room temperature).

Ingredients

2 oranges
2 bunches rhubarb, stems trimmed, washed and cut into bite-sized pieces
½ cup sugar
4 pears, peeled, cored and diced
1 punnet raspberries
icing sugar, for dusting (optional)

Crumble topping
75 g butter
⅓ cup sugar
½ cup plain flour
1 cup roughly chopped nuts
½ teaspoon ground cinnamon

Method

1 Preheat the oven to 200°C.

2 Wash one of the oranges and cut it into small dice, skin and all, retaining the juices but discarding any pips. Transfer to a large saucepan with any juices, add the rhubarb and sprinkle the sugar over. Squeeze over the juice of the other orange and mix until well combined.

3 Place the saucepan over medium heat and simmer for at least 10 minutes – it will turn into a hot-pink syrupy stew. Spoon into a 5 cm deep ovenproof dish and add the other fruit.

4 To make the crumble topping, place the butter, sugar and flour in a large bowl and rub together with your fingers to form crumbs. Add the nuts and cinnamon and mix well, then crumble over the fruit.

5 Bake for about 20 minutes until the fruit is bubbling and the topping is golden. If I'm serving the crumble at the table, I sprinkle a light dusting of icing sugar over the top.

Serves 8

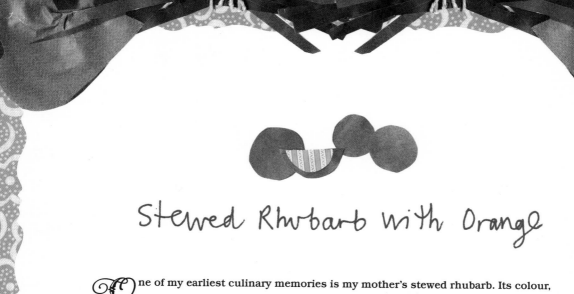

Stewed Rhubarb with Orange

One of my earliest culinary memories is my mother's stewed rhubarb. Its colour, texture and slightly tart flavour is unlike any other vegetable. Vegetable, you say? It's a common misconception that rhubarb is a fruit – it is most definitely a vegetable.

When my mother stewed rhubarb she would use some of it to make a generous pie, with enough left over to store in a large jar in the fridge to have with cream or ice cream later. I also love stewed rhubarb for breakfast with a good Greek yoghurt or spooned over Bircher muesli. One thing to remember is that the leaves of common garden rhubarb are poisonous – it's only the stems that are edible.

Method

1 Wash one of the oranges and cut it into 1 cm dice, skin and all, retaining the juices but discarding any pips. Transfer to a large saucepan with any juices, add the rhubarb and sprinkle the sugar over. Squeeze in the juice of the other orange and mix until well combined. Place the pan over high heat, stirring until the sugar has dissolved.

2 When the mixture starts to bubble, give it a good stir then reduce the heat to a low simmer, cover and cook for 20 minutes – it will transform into a hot-pink frothy syrup.

3 Serve just as it is, or with cream, yoghurt or ice cream.

Serves 6

Ingredients

2 oranges

2 bunches rhubarb, stems trimmed, washed and cut into 3 cm lengths

1 cup sugar

pouring cream, whipped cream, yoghurt or good strawberry ice cream, to serve (optional)

Ah, ginger. It's a sultry word that conjures up heat, spice and all things exotic. For the Chinese, ginger has medicinal properties: it is said to promote circulation, reduce inflammation and open the pores. For the Europeans, the appearance of fresh ginger signals the arrival of winter and it is fermented to make alcoholic drinks, and in Germany they use dried ginger to flavour cakes and pastries. The Japanese and Burmese pickle ginger to use as an accompaniment to a variety of dishes, while other Asian cultures use it to flavour steamed fish and chicken, and in countless variations of stir-fries and curries. Australians have preserved and candied this versatile spice since it was first introduced into our cuisine.

I use ginger in so many ways. I like to combine freshly grated ginger with lime juice and olive oil to make a dressing that really brings a salad to life. I love it in chicken soup, where it adds an extra dimension to the flavour. Japanese-style pickled ginger served with salted cashew nuts is one of my favourite nibbles to serve with drinks, and crystallised ginger always has a home in my pantry, especially when dipped in good-quality dark chocolate. I also add freshly grated ginger to boiling water and honey to make a drink to soothe a sore throat.

The warm familiarity of this spice is inherently comforting – it should be a staple in everyone's kitchen. Opposite is one of my favourite ginger recipes ever: a true classic.

GINGER!

GINGER NUTS

Makes at least 40

I have always been wild about ginger nuts, even though I have broken teeth crunching into them and disgusted many a boyfriend by dunking them in my tea. This recipe is from the thirties, and it has stood the test of time admirably. The only change I have made is to replace the shortening with butter, and the cocoa with allspice (it adds a lovely peppery flavour). These biscuits are not as hard as commercial ginger nuts, and if you don't squish them flat before baking they turn out like chunky chocolate-chip cookies.

For a fun dessert, I whip 600 ml cream with 2 tablespoons caster sugar and, when the biscuits have cooled completely, I sandwich them together with this mixture to form a caterpillar. I then refrigerate it overnight, splash some of my favourite liqueur over the top and chill for a few more hours, then melt 250 g dark chocolate and drizzle it over the caterpillar in fine lines.

Method

1 Cream the butter and sugar together until fluffy. Gently warm the golden syrup in a saucepan until runny. In another saucepan, heat the milk to just below boiling point and add the bicarbonate of soda – it should be a nice frothy consistency. Now for some kitchen chemistry: add the milk to the golden syrup and watch it foam (I always get a kick out of this bit!).

2 Sift the dry ingredients into the creamed butter and sugar. With a spatula or wooden spoon, fold in the golden syrup mixture until it becomes a thick dough, then cover and refrigerate for 30 minutes. While you wait, butter or line three baking trays and preheat the oven to 180˚C.

3 Take a spoonful of the chilled mixture and roll it into a ball between the palms of your hands. Place it on the tray and press into whatever shape you prefer. Repeat with the remaining mixture, leaving plenty of room for spreading. Bake for about 20 minutes. I always know my cookies are done by the delicious smell that creeps through the house.

Ingredients

250 g butter

1¼ cups dark brown sugar

1 cup golden syrup

2 tablespoons milk

2 teaspoons bicarbonate of soda

4 cups plain flour

pinch salt

¼ teaspoon ground allspice

1 tablespoon ground cinnamon

2 heaped tablespoons ground ginger

rice

Coming from a Spanish family that lived in the Philippines, we were always surrounded by rice – it was a big part of our culinary rituals. As far back as I can remember there was a large rice cooker in the corner of our kitchen, and it was used every day. The leftovers from dinner were eaten for breakfast or fried up for afternoon tea the next day.

Apart from being an everyday staple, rice also featured on special occasions. My Grandma Mary's *bibingka malagkit* (a sweet sticky rice dish cooked in a banana leaf) was particularly prized. This traditional Filipino dessert would always sit proudly on the table at family celebrations, and we'd all make sure we ate our main meal quickly so that we'd get to it faster.

Perfectly cooked rice is so simple – if you follow these few basic rules you can't go wrong. I use the absorption method, which can be adapted to a rice cooker or cooking on the stovetop in a saucepan with a lid. Once mastered, you'll never make bad rice again.

This method is for regular white rice – for brown and wild rice you'll need to increase the cooking time to 20 minutes.

(The lowdown on seasoning: rice will absorb the flavours of whatever you serve it with, so as a general rule, try and keep it simple. I usually just add a pinch of salt and a bay leaf to the rice before I cook it. You could also add lemon zest, or if you are serving duck or a Thai-flavoured dish, try star anise or a few cardamom pods.)

1 To work out how much rice to cook, calculate ½–¾ cup per person. This is on the generous side, but it is better to have too much than not enough.

2 Put the rice in a saucepan with a tight-fitting lid or in a rice cooker and cover with cold water. Swish the rice around in the water to rinse, and then slowly pour the water out (being careful not to lose any rice down the sink).

3 Tap the sides of the pan or cooker to allow the rice to settle evenly, then place your middle fingertip directly on the surface of the rice and fill the pan with water up to your finger's first joint.

4 If you're using a rice cooker, switch it on. If you're cooking on the stove, bring the water to a boil then turn the heat down to the lowest setting, cover and cook for 10–12 minutes. Most importantly: do not stir!

5 Leave covered until ready to serve.

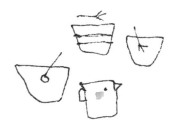

Fried Eggs & Rice
Ode to Nestor

Serves 4

ather's Day falls right at the start of spring, but instead of feeling energised by the coming season, I'm usually a bit down in the dumps as I'm thinking of my lovely dad, Nestor, and how much I miss him. When it came to cooking, Dad had a small but strong repertoire of tried-and-true dishes, but the recipe of his that I make most often is fried eggs and rice. His version always contained canned corned beef, which he would shred and fry with the eggs. Having lived through the Second World War in the Philippines, Dad retained a certain fondness for canned produce, especially Tang, a reconstituted orange-flavoured powdered drink, and his beloved canned corned beef.

This recipe is simple and delicious just as it is, but you can spice it up a bit by adding a few extra ingredients. For an Asian flavour, fry some finely chopped spring onions with some sliced Chinese pork sausage before you add the rice. For a Spanish feel, fry a chopped chorizo or *morcilla* (Spanish blood sausage) with half a finely chopped red onion until the onion has softened, then add the rice.

With or without the canned meat or other variations, this meal is the perfect hangover cure and makes for great comfort food. If I ever come home to an empty house and want to cook something quick, easy and nourishing, this is the dish I turn to.

Method

1 Heat half the oil in a heavy-based frying pan and toss in the rice. Fry for a minute or two until slightly crunchy, then season and transfer to a plate.

2 Add the remaining oil to the pan, increase the heat to medium and fry the eggs. When the edges start to curl and turn golden, add a drop of water to the pan then cover and cook for about 15 seconds, so that the whites are just set but the yolks are still runny. Season with salt and pepper, then scoop the eggs out gently with a spatula or egg slice and place on top of the cooked rice. Serve sprinkled with Tabasco sauce.

Ingredients

2 tablespoons olive oil

2 cups cold cooked rice

sea salt and freshly
ground black pepper

8 eggs, preferably
free-range

Tabasco sauce, to serve

*My family &
other animals*

Asparagus

From a very early age, I have been mesmerised by the handsome asparagus. As a child, I remember my mother hiring a hypnotist to persuade my brother Ignatius to eat the noble spears – she was so crazy about them that she could not bear the thought of a child of hers growing up without a passion for this unique vegetable. (The hypnotist did the trick – my brother is now a dedicated asparagus-lover!) On my first trip to Spain, when I was twenty-one, I stood gobsmacked in front of a stand of wild asparagus in the grand old corridors of the *Mercado de Chamartin* (Madrid's finest food market). Although wild asparagus is thin and reedy, I just had to buy a bunch and all day long I nibbled the raw sweet tips. When I returned home that night I was left with nothing but the feathery foliage and, of course, unmistakeably aromatic asparagus wee.

The French are particularly fond of thick, white asparagus known as *spargel*. Grown in a controlled environment and deprived of light, this is considered a delicacy. In Australia, I've only ever seen it in jars at delicatessens or very rarely at my greengrocers at the beginning of autumn. It can be steamed but, depending on their age and thickness, they may require a little more time to cook as they're generally much thicker than green asparagus. The Italians have developed their own variety called *Violetto d'Albenga*. These purple spears are not widely available in Australia, but are certainly worth trying if you come across them. It requires less steaming time than green asparagus and is delicious baked.

The most readily available asparagus in Australia is the green variety, which is high in fibre, potassium and folic acid and acts as a diuretic. I eat it steamed, baked, boiled, grilled, barbecued and raw: I'm still not sure which I like best, but here are a couple of simple options for you to try.

Grilled Asparagus Salad

This is a great salad to serve with grilled fish or beef.

Ingredients

3 bunches asparagus, woody ends discarded
olive oil, for brushing
sea salt and freshly ground black pepper
4 hardboiled eggs, peeled and cut in half lengthways, yolks separated from whites
¼ cup finely grated parmesan cheese
¼ cup finely crushed roasted almonds or cashews
pinch paprika
extra virgin olive oil, for drizzling
1 tablespoon vinegar (red-wine, sherry or balsamic)

Method

1 Preheat the grill to high. Cover a baking tray with foil and lay out the asparagus in a single layer. Lightly brush each spear with olive oil and season.

2 Grill the asparagus for about 4 minutes then turn the spears over and brush oil over the other side. Grill for a further 3 minutes until the spears are cooked but still slightly crunchy, then set them aside.

3 Sieve the egg yolks into a bowl, then sieve the whites into the same bowl. Add the parmesan, crushed nuts, paprika and some salt and pepper and gently toss together.

4 Transfer the cooked asparagus to a bowl, drizzle over the extra virgin olive oil and vinegar and toss to combine. Add the sieved egg and parmesan mixture and gently mix together before serving on a platter.

Serves 6

Steamed Asparagus

Steamed asparagus is the perfect partner to a garlicky aïoli (see Mayonnaise recipe on page 6). To turn it into an elegant entrée or side dish, smother it in butter, season and top with shaved parmesan and lemon juice.

The secret to perfect steamed asparagus is to get the freshest asparagus you can find and cook it straight away. I use an asparagus steamer, which cooks the spears in an upright position so the delicate tips are further from the heat. However, if you don't own one of these brilliant cooking devices you can improvise with a small saucepan, some cooking twine and some foil – it sounds complicated but is actually really simple, and is a great way to cook asparagus evenly.

Ingredients

1 bunch asparagus, woody ends discarded

Method

1 Tie the spears into a bundle with some cooking twine or thread. Stand the bundle in a small saucepan and add water to a depth of about 5 cm. Cut out a piece of foil large enough to cover the bundle, and seal around the rim of the saucepan, creating a teepee-like structure.

2 Bring the water to a boil and steam the asparagus for a few minutes, then test by removing a spear from the bundle and bending at the stem – if it snaps off, it's perfect.

Serves 4 as a side dish

DUCK PANCAKES

Duck pancakes served with lychee daiquiris have long been a family favourite of ours and have kicked off many a Christmas party. My mother has made these pancakes for us since we were very young – they are always a hit with kids.

It's quickest and easiest to get your duck from an Asian grocer or a Chinatown if you live near one. Ask them to cut it up for you – it will save you a lot of mess and stress.

Ingredients

2 bunches spring onions, trimmed to about 10 cm long

1 Chinese barbecued duck, chopped into pieces, meat and skin shredded

1 cup hoisin sauce or sweet bean paste

8–10 Chinese pancakes

1 bunch coriander (optional)

Method

1 With a very sharp knife, make 2 cm-long cuts into the stem ends of the spring onions, then drop them into a bowl of iced water for about 20 minutes – this will make the ends curl dramatically.

2 Arrange the duck, spring onions and sauce or paste on a large serving platter. Soften the pancakes by dipping each one in boiling water for about 10 seconds.

3 Invite your guests to take a pancake and fill it with a piece of spring onion, a drizzle of sauce or paste and some duck skin and meat, then fold one end and roll up the pancake (one end should remain open with the ingredients sticking out).

Serves 4

MON CHEW'S WONTONS

My family was well-known for the delicious empanadas we would have on special occasions. They are a cross between a pastie and a dumpling, and were either deep-fried or baked. Although I liked them, I found they were quite filling and would take up far too much room in my stomach before I had a chance to taste all the other delicious things on offer!

When I met Lil's girlfriend, Mon Chew, I learned that her family's equivalent of the empanada was the light and crisp wonton. These would be produced by the dozen for family celebrations, and Mon's dextrous hands have folded countless numbers of these tiny parcels of treasure over the years. This is her family recipe – you can either fry them, or boil them for a slightly healthier option.

Method

1 Put the pork mince, spring onion, soy sauce, sesame oil and a generous grinding of black pepper in a large bowl. Crack the egg over and mix with your hands to evenly distribute all the ingredients.

2 Take one wonton wrapper and put half a teaspoon of pork mixture in the centre. Fold the wrapper in half diagonally, then bring the other corners together to form a bundle. Brush the inside of the top of the wrapper with water and press together to seal – it's important to seal them properly so they don't burst open when deep-fried. Transfer to a plate and continue with the rest of the mixture (but don't stack the wontons too close together on the plate or they'll stick to each other).

3 In a large frying pan, add vegetable oil to a depth of about 4 cm (or enough to cover the wontons) and heat over medium heat. When the oil is hot but not smoking, fry the wontons in batches for 4–5 minutes (check that they are cooked by slicing one open – if the pork mince has no trace of pink, they are ready). Alternatively, you could boil the wontons in batches in a large pan of water for 5 minutes.

4 Serve the wontons on a large platter with some sweet chilli sauce for dipping.

Makes 40 wontons

Ingredients

200 g pork mince

6 spring onions,
   finely sliced

2 tablespoons soy sauce

¾ tablespoon sesame oil

freshly ground
   black pepper

1 egg

40 wonton wrappers

vegetable oil, for frying

sweet chilli sauce,
   to serve

*My family &
other animals*

CHUN CHEW'S
HAINAN CHICKEN RICE

When we adopted Mon Chew into our clan, her family were also welcomed with open arms and willing tastebuds. Mon's mother Chun makes the best Hainan chicken ever, and has generously allowed her family recipe to be included in this book.

This traditional Chinese method, where the residual heat of the water cooks the chicken, gives the meat a beautiful soft, silky texture. Although this might seem like a daunting recipe, it is actually very simple once you begin, and the combination of textures and subtle, pure flavours is very satisfying. The leftovers are especially delicious in sandwiches the next day.

Ingredients

1 × 1.6 kg chicken, rinsed, excess fat removed from the cavity

1 red onion, diced

2 tablespoons olive oil

dash light soy sauce

1 × 4 cm knob ginger, peeled and thinly sliced

½ brown onion, diced

4 cups rice, rinsed and drained

1 chicken stock cube *or* 1 teaspoon chicken stock powder (optional)

¼ teaspoon salt

1 bunch gai lan (Chinese broccoli), trimmed

chopped coriander, to garnish

My family &
other animals

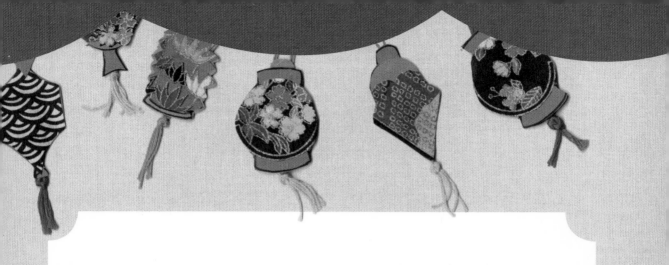

Method

1 Choose a stockpot large enough to hold the chicken, fill with water and bring to a boil.

2 Immerse the chicken in the boiling water, pushing it down with a wooden spoon to fill the cavity with water. Bring the water back to a boil, then simmer over the lowest possible heat for 10 minutes before turning off the heat. Cover and leave to stand for 45 minutes.

3 Meanwhile, place the diced red onion in a small heatproof bowl. In a heavy-based frying pan, heat the olive oil then pour three-quarters of it over the onion. Add a dash of light soy sauce to the onion mixture and leave to stand.

4 Fry the ginger and diced brown onion in the remaining olive oil over medium heat, stirring to ensure they are evenly coated in oil. When the onion is soft, add the rice and fry for about 5 minutes. Add the stock cube or powder if using and the salt, and continue to fry for about 5 minutes until the rice dries out a bit.

5 Remove the chicken from the stockpot, reserving the stock. Rinse the chicken under cold water inside and out to cool it completely, then set it aside for 30 minutes to drain, making sure there is no water left inside the chicken.

6 Transfer the rice to a saucepan and place your middle fingertip directly on the surface of the rice. Fill the pan with stock up to your finger's first joint. Bring to a boil then turn the heat down to the lowest setting, cover and cook for 10–12 minutes.

7 Bring the remaining chicken stock to a simmer, and drop the gai lan into the hot stock for 30 seconds – 1 minute to blanch. Remove and cut each piece into three lengths.

8 Cut the chicken into pieces and serve on a bed of steamed rice with some gai lan to the side. Spoon some of the red-onion mixture over the chicken and rice and sprinkle some coriander on top.

Serves 6

COCA MALLORQUINA
(SPANISH PIZZA)

This recipe for Spanish pizza originated in Mallorca – although, unlike pizza, *coca* never contains cheese. Because it is served at room temperature, it is the perfect dish to take on a picnic. It's sensational with a glass of tempranillo or a good sangria.

Ingredients

2 tablespoons olive oil

3 cloves garlic, crushed

3 white or brown onions, chopped

3 large red capsicums, white insides and seeds removed, finely chopped

8 tomatoes, roughly chopped

2 medium-sized eggplants, cubed

Pizza dough

1 × 8 g sachet yeast

1 teaspoon sugar

2 tablespoons olive oil

2 cups plain flour, plus extra if required

1 teaspoon salt

½ teaspoon freshly ground black pepper

Method

1 To make the dough, dissolve the yeast and sugar in 1 cup warm water and leave for 10 minutes or until bubbles appear. Butter a large baking tray and set aside.

2 Add the olive oil, flour, salt and pepper to the yeast mixture and knead to form a smooth, soft ball of dough, adding more flour if needed. Transfer to a well-oiled deep bowl and leave to stand in a warm place for at least 10 minutes, or until the mixture has doubled in volume. Preheat the oven to 200°C.

3 Turn the dough out onto a floured bench and flatten by hand into a round about 2 cm thick. Transfer to the prepared baking tray and leave to stand for another 10 minutes.

4 Meanwhile, in a large, heavy-based saucepan, heat the olive oil over medium heat then add the garlic and onion. Reduce the heat to low and cook until the onion has softened. Add the capsicum, cover and cook for 5 minutes.

5 Add the tomato and eggplant to the pan and cook, uncovered, for a further 10 minutes.

6 Spread this topping evenly over the dough and bake for about 20 minutes, or until the crust is golden brown, then serve at room temperature.

Serves 6

Fennel, Olive &
Blood-orange Salad

My dear friend Meredith, who is responsible for the captivating watercolours in this book, has a real love of life and an appreciation for the everyday objects that surround her. When she was living above my shop, I would often hear her singing away as she worked on huge canvasses or tiny intricate figures. Finding her the perfect vintage jug, teacup or plate for inspiration guaranteed me a seat at her table, with beautiful food and fine conversation.

After telling her one day how much I loved fennel, she whipped up this perfect salad for me. Teamed with pungent, slightly bitter green olives and the sweet, summery blood oranges, the strong refreshing flavour of fennel really shines through. I like to serve this salad with a subtle-tasting cheese like *manchego* or provolone, and some slices of prosciutto on the side.

Ingredients

1 large fennel bulb or 2 small
  fennel bulbs, trimmed and
  sliced diagonally into 1 cm
  pieces (feathery leaves reserved
  for garnish)

1 cup large green olives,
  drained of excess oil

2 blood oranges, peel and pith
  removed, broken into segments

1 radicchio, leaves separated

½ bag mixed salad greens,
  well washed

2 small cucumbers, peeled and sliced

Dressing

1 clove garlic, finely chopped with
  ½ teaspoon salt and ½ teaspoon sugar
  to make a paste

⅓ cup extra virgin olive oil

1 tablespoon apple-cider vinegar

juice of 1 blood orange
  (about 2 tablespoons)

freshly ground black pepper

2 tablespoons finely chopped flat-leaf
  parsley (optional)

Method

1 Place the fennel slices in a bowl, cover with iced water and soak for 10 minutes.

2 To make the dressing, mix all the ingredients together.

3 Drain the fennel and toss with the remaining ingredients in a large salad bowl, then mix through the dressing.

Serves 4 as an entrée

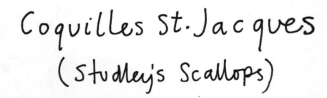

Coquilles St. Jacques
(Studley's Scallops)

One of the most knowledgeable, humorous, elegant and gentle souls I know is Studley Lush, a dear friend of mine. We met years ago at an antiques auction where we were both bargain-hunting, and I now turn to him whenever I want to know anything about antique clocks, silver, crockery or politics, or if I'm in need of a good joke (which is often).

Studley is the proud father of triplets – all girls – now in their thirties and with children of their own. I always say that the mark of a good parent is how much your children think of you once they have their kids, and Studley is revered by his girls and grandkids for his wicked wit and loving nature. He is a real family man, and that's why I asked him for his favourite family recipe – in true Studley form, he gave me four. This one is a winner.

Ingredients

75 g butter

600 g fresh scallops, roe removed, cut in half

1 bacon rasher, rind removed, finely chopped

150 g button mushrooms, thinly sliced

2 tablespoons plain flour

300 ml milk

200 g grated cheese

4 spring onions, finely chopped

1 teaspoon freshly ground black pepper

100 g freshly grated parmesan cheese

Method

1 In a large, heavy-based pan, melt 25 g of the butter over high heat then sear the scallops quickly on both sides. Remove from the pan and set aside.

2 Add the bacon and mushrooms to the pan and fry for 5 minutes, then set them aside with the scallops.

3 Melt the remaining butter in the pan over medium heat then stir in the flour until you have a sandy texture. Gradually add the milk, stirring after each addition, until you have a thick, smooth sauce.

4 Stir in the cheese until combined, then gently mix in the reserved bacon, mushrooms and scallops, along with the spring onions and black pepper, then remove from the heat.

5 Transfer the mixture into six individual ovenproof dishes and liberally sprinkle parmesan cheese over each one. Place under a hot grill until the tops are nicely browned.

Serves 6 as an entrée

Mouclade with White Wine, Cream & Leeks

This recipe was another that I created for the black-and-pink themed dinner party I threw for my future husband Simon when we first met. I wanted the sauce to be an inviting rich pink – enter my brother Ignatius wielding a bottle of rosé and a spicy chorizo, and this became a real show-stopper.

Method

1 In a large pot with a lid, combine the mussels, parsley, rosemary, bay leaves, leek tops, black peppercorns and 2 cloves of the crushed garlic, and pour in the bottle of Riesling. Cover and bring to a boil, simmering for about 5 minutes or until all the mussels have opened.

2 Remove from the heat and leave to cool for a few minutes before draining the mussels in a colander, reserving the cooking liquid and discarding the herbs and flavourings. Discard any mussels that have not opened and carefully remove the beards (I find a little pair of nail scissors very handy for this job). Place them in a bowl and set aside.

3 In a heavy-based saucepan over medium heat, melt 60 g of the butter and fry the sliced leeks for 5 minutes. Reduce the heat to low, add the remaining butter and the garlic, cover and fry for 5 minutes.

4 Increase the heat to medium and add the mussel-cooking liquid. Simmer for 10 minutes to reduce a little, then add the rosé wine and simmer for another 5 minutes.

5 In a bowl, whisk the egg yolks and cream together. Pour ¼ cup of the simmering sauce into the cream mixture and whisk gently to combine. Add the crushed pink peppercorns and another ¼ cup of the simmering sauce and whisk again. Pour the cream mixture into the saucepan and reduce the heat to low. Add the sliced chorizo and simmer on low for 5 minutes, stirring continuously, then season with salt.

6 Serve the mussels with the sauce and chopped herbs sprinkled over. Eat with plenty of crusty bread.

Serves 8

Ingredients

2 kg fresh black mussels, lightly scrubbed with steel wool then rinsed

1 bunch flat-leaf parsley, finely chopped

2 large sprigs rosemary

4 bay leaves

4 leeks, tops trimmed and reserved, white parts well washed and finely sliced

1 teaspoon black peppercorns

4 cloves garlic, crushed

1 × 750 ml bottle Riesling

80 g butter

500 ml rosé wine

2 egg yolks, lightly beaten

600 ml thickened cream

1 teaspoon pink peppercorns, crushed

2 chorizos, sliced

sea salt

finely chopped flat-leaf parsley or chervil, to garnish

crusty bread, to serve

Apricot Torte

This is my mum Margot's most-used recipe, always made with lots of love. It was handed down to her from my Grandma Mary, and my whole life it has been something of a family secret, so I'm honoured to be able to include it here. This is an Italian-style torte that Margot makes with either apricot or blueberry jam (if you're using blueberry jam, the addition of 1 cup of fresh blueberries is sensational).

Ingredients

240 g butter
1 cup sugar
3 egg yolks
1 teaspoon
   vanilla extract
2½ cups plain flour
1 × 500 g jar
   apricot jam
handful
   blanched almonds

Method

1 In an electric mixer or food processor, cream the butter and sugar until fluffy, then add the egg yolks and vanilla and mix until combined. Gradually add the flour, mixing between each addition.

2 When the dough pulls away from the sides of the bowl, transfer it to a floured surface and roll it into a ball. Cover with plastic film or greaseproof paper and chill in the fridge for 1 hour.

3 Preheat the oven to 180°C and butter a 24 cm diameter pie dish or flan tin. On a floured surface, roll out the pastry to fit the dish, saving about a quarter of the dough for the trimmings. Line the dish with the pastry then spread with a ½ cm layer of apricot jam.

4 Roll the remaining pastry into thin strips and lay them across the jam in a criss-cross pattern. Dot the middle of each diamond with an almond, then bake for 40–50 minutes. Cut into squares before serving.

Makes about 24

*My family &
other animals*

Blueberry Muffins

We call my mum Margot 'Queen of the Blueberry', as she has owned a blueberry farm on Sydney's Central Coast for over 25 years. Throughout her childhood, my daughter Lil spent a lot of time there, picking, planting and most of all, baking. I suspect her finely tuned palate is a result of all the culinary treats my mother exposed her to at a young age!

When I asked Lil what her favourite recipe of Margot's was, she replied emphatically, 'Her blueberry muffins, of course!' So here they are – apparently the secret is rolling the muffins in sugar just before they cool completely.

Method

1 Preheat the oven to 200°C, butter two muffin tins well and sprinkle with flour. Mix all the dry ingredients in a large bowl and set aside.

2 Mix the lemon zest, eggs, milk, yoghurt and vegetable oil in a separate bowl, then make a well in the dry ingredients and pour in the liquid. Add the blueberries and mix well to combine.

3 Pour the mixture into muffin tins and bake for about 25 minutes or until golden. Remove from the oven and, when almost cool, remove the muffins from the tins and roll them in caster sugar.

Makes about 24

Ingredients

2½ cups plain flour
1 cup self-raising flour
2 teaspoons bicarbonate of soda
1 teaspoon salt
⅔ cup sugar
1 teaspoon finely grated lemon zest
3 eggs, beaten
1¼ cups milk
1¼ cups plain yoghurt
⅔ cup vegetable oil
2 cups blueberries
caster sugar, to serve

*My family &
other animals*

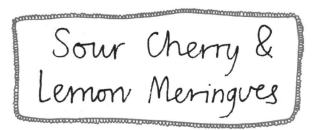

Sour Cherry & Lemon Meringues

One rainy Saturday morning, as I was depositing some veggie scraps into the worm farm in my backyard, I heard whispers and giggling coming from over the fence and I noticed a large broom waving around in my lemon tree. As my dog Lola began to bark, I snapped off a great big branch laden with lemons and stuck my head over the fence, hoping to catch the thieves red-handed and embarrass them with my generosity. To my surprise, there stood two nuns from the neighbouring school, apparently on a mission to make lemon curd. I cheekily reminded them of the eighth commandment, and proffered my branch of lemons.

Early the next morning I answered a knock at the front door, and there stood one of the nuns with a jar of fresh lemon curd for me. It was so delicious that I was inspired to incorporate it into one of my Grandma Mary's classic desserts. If you can, make the meringues the night before so they have time to cool and set completely before you add the filling.

Ingredients

8 eggwhites, at
   room temperature
1½ cups sugar
1 tablespoon vanilla extract
   or lemon juice
1 cup desiccated coconut
300 ml thickened
   cream whipped with
   2 tablespoons sugar and
   1 teaspoon vanilla extract
1 cup sour cherries
Limoncello or Kirsch,
   to serve (optional)

Lemon curd

juice and finely grated
   zest of 3 lemons
120 g unsalted butter
⅔ cup sugar
4 eggs

Method

1 Preheat the oven to 160°C and line two large baking trays with greaseproof paper. Beat the eggwhites in an electric mixer until they begin to stiffen. Gradually add the sugar, beating between each addition, then the vanilla or lemon juice, and mix until stiff peaks form.

2 Fold in the coconut, then spoon the meringue into a piping bag with a large nozzle and pipe out a flat 6 cm-diameter disc topped with two rings (in a vol-au-vent shape). Continue until all the mixture is used, then cook for 45 minutes (check after 15 minutes: if they have started to brown, turn the oven down to 150°C).

3 Meanwhile, make the lemon curd by combining the lemon juice, zest, butter and sugar in a heavy-based saucepan over medium heat, and stirring constantly for about 2 minutes. As the butter melts it will become frothy. When all the in-gredients are combined and the sugar is completely dissolved, remove the pan from the heat and transfer the mixture to a jug or small bowl and leave to cool for about 5 minutes.

4 Beat the eggs, then strain them through a sieve into a large bowl. Wash the sieve well to remove all traces of egg, then strain the cooled lemon mixture into the egg and mix thoroughly. Strain the combined mixture back into the pan you melted the butter in (no need to clean the sieve this time) and cook over low–medium heat, stirring with a wooden spoon until the mixture thickens. This process takes a few minutes – just keep stirring but don't let the mixture boil or the eggs will separate. As soon as the mixture has thickened, remove the pan from the heat and set aside.

5 When the meringues have cooled slightly, fill each one with a tablespoon of lemon curd and a tablespoon of whipped cream, then finish with a few sour cherries. If you want to be really decadent, drizzle a little Limoncello or Kirsch over the whole lot.

Makes at least 10

Grandma Mary's Carrot Cake

On my first trip to California, when I was 17, carrot cake was all the rage. I was travelling with Grandma Mary, who is half-American, and she was thrilled to be spending time with her sisters and their families. One of Grandma's nieces, Mary Duree, is a fabulous cook, and during the two months we stayed with her I gained 20 kg! This scrumptious carrot cake is a special memory from that lovely summer.

Ingredients

2 cups plain flour
2 teaspoons baking powder
2 teaspoons
  ground cinnamon
1 teaspoon salt
4 eggs
1½ cups sugar
1 tablespoon vanilla extract
1½ cups vegetable oil
3 cups grated carrot
½ cup sultanas
½ cup chopped
  walnuts or pecans

Cream cheese icing
250 g cream cheese
150 g unsalted butter,
  softened
500 g icing sugar
juice and finely grated
  zest of 1 lemon
1 teaspoon vanilla extract

Method

1 Preheat the oven to 180°C, butter a deep 22 cm cake tin and line the base with greaseproof paper. Sift the flour, baking powder, cinnamon and salt together.

2 Beat the eggs until thick and creamy in an electric mixer. Slowly add the sugar while still beating, then the vanilla. Transfer the mixture to a large bowl and add alternate batches of the flour mixture and vegetable oil, mixing with a wooden spoon between each addition. When all the ingredients are evenly blended, fold in the grated carrot, sultanas and chopped nuts with a whisk.

3 Spoon the mixture into the tin and bake on the middle shelf of the oven for 40 minutes. Check by inserting a skewer in the middle of the cake – if it comes out clean, it's done; if not, bake for another 5 minutes or so.

4 To make the icing, beat the cream cheese and butter together until well combined. Sift the icing sugar over and gently fold through with a spatula, then beat until smooth. Add the lemon juice, zest and vanilla and mix until well combined.

5 Allow the cake to cool in the tin for a few minutes, then turn out onto a wire rack to cool completely. When cold, cover generously with cream cheese icing.

Serves 12

Meredith's Prune, Fig & Chocolate Cake

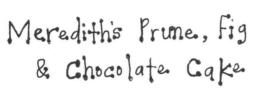

When I first began work on this book, I was determined to include a cake that my friend Meredith could enjoy – she is a coeliac. The challenge was on to create something with all her favourite ingredients and not a hint of gluten: the result is this dark, moist, almost panforte-like cake.

Method

1 The night before you want to make the cake, soak the prunes and figs overnight in the boiling water. If you forget to do this and you're running out of time, put the dried fruit in a saucepan with the water and simmer for about 5 minutes until tender, then set aside to cool.

2 Melt the chocolate bits in a heatproof bowl that fits snugly over a saucepan of boiling water, then set aside to cool.

3 Preheat the oven to 180°C. Butter a 25 cm springform cake tin and line the base and sides with greaseproof paper.

4 Cream the butter and sugar in an electric mixer until light and fluffy then gradually add the beaten egg, scraping down the sides of the bowl as you go. Add the remaining ingredients and mix until evenly blended (but don't overbeat).

5 Pour the batter into the tin and bake for 30 minutes. See if it's ready by lightly pressing the top – if it springs back, it's done. Allow the cake to cool in the tin for a few minutes, then turn out onto a wire rack to cool completely.

6 While the cake is cooling, combine all the icing ingredients and mix until smooth and creamy, then spread generously over the cake. It will stay moist for days.

Serves 10

Ingredients

250 g dried prunes, pitted

250 g dried figs

2 cups boiling water

1 cup dark chocolate bits

250 g butter

1 cup demerara sugar

6 eggs, lightly beaten

1 tablespoon vanilla extract

250 g ground almonds

1 teaspoon bicarbonate of soda

1 teaspoon ground cinnamon

1 teaspoon ground cloves

1 teaspoon ground nutmeg

Icing

3 cups icing sugar

250 g cream cheese (or mascarpone with 1 tablespoon crème fraîche added)

40 g butter

2 tablespoons tawny port or Armagnac

1 teaspoon vanilla extract

3 drops almond essence

Rev Bev's ✝ Refrigerator Cake

FROM LIL: This delicious biscuity cake is a tradition in my dad's family. My kaftan-wearing grandma Beverley, known to us as Rev Bev since she became a Reverend of the Uniting Church, first made this in 1970 for a fundraiser at my father's pre-school, and it proved so popular that from then on it became the centrepiece at family birthday celebrations.

As with all family traditions, there are a few unspoken rules surrounding this recipe. The first time I made it was for my father's 40th birthday, and every aficionado of Rev Bev's original cake was there. Although my father was touched that I had chosen to make it for him, he was quick to point out that it was still a little crunchy and would be best left for a day before eating. This was reiterated by several family members – in fact, it was only the ever-kind and unobtrusive Rev Bev who refrained from passing any comment on my efforts.

Nonetheless, there wasn't a piece left, and now it has become a tradition for a new generation. I always double the quantities of this recipe for parties – any leftover almond filling can be frozen and kept for when you make it again. To uphold the tradition, leave the cake to sit in the fridge for a day before you serve it (this makes the filling merge with the cake in a delicious, gooey mess). I often serve this covered in chocolate-dipped cherries, strawberries and biscotti, but it's fabulous on its own.

Method

1 Butter a lamington tin and line with a large sheet of foil, leaving enough overhang on each side to fold over and cover the cake.

2 In an electric mixer, cream the butter and sugar until light and fluffy, then add the egg yolks, almond meal and vanilla and mix to combine. Add the milk and continue mixing to a thick, creamy consistency. Beat the eggwhites until stiff peaks form and fold into the mixture before setting aside.

3 Pour some more milk into a small bowl and add a generous dash of the rum or liqueur. Dip the biscuits in one at a time, leaving them just long enough to soak up some liquid but taking them out before they fall apart.

4 Lay one third of the soaked biscuits in the lamington tin, making sure the base is completely covered. Add half the almond mixture in an even layer, then add another layer of soaked biscuits. Add the rest of the almond mixture then finish with another layer of biscuits. Fold over the foil to cover the cake and leave in the fridge overnight.

5 Not long before serving, remove the tin from the fridge, peel back the foil and turn the cake out onto a platter. Remove foil and spread the whipped cream all over the top and sides of the cake. Return it to the fridge until ready to serve.

Serves at least 8

Ingredients

125 g butter

125 g caster sugar

2 eggs, separated

125 g almond meal

½ teaspoon vanilla extract

¼ cup milk, plus extra for dunking

sweet rum or liqueur (I use Cointreau or Licor 43), for dunking

1 × 400 g packet Nice biscuits

300 ml thickened cream whipped with ½ teaspoon vanilla extract and 1 tablespoon caster sugar

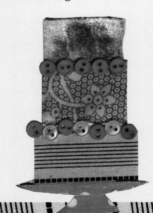

Sans Rival

When my beautiful Grandma Mary turned 100, this monumental occasion was marked with a card from both the President of the United States and Queen Elizabeth, though it was her family who truly celebrated her amazing life.

Grandma Mary has lived the life of about three people. Born in 1908, she has seen eighteen American presidents, endured the ravages of the First World War and survived the Second World War. She was the second daughter of five, and in 1912, when her mother died of diphtheria, she was thrown into the job of caring and cooking for the family, including her youngest sister, Dorothy, who was only eight months old at the time.

She became a creative and accomplished cook, and out of all the wonderful recipes that she tried over the years, this cake is what everyone asks for time and time again. Literally meaning 'without rival', this majestic creation would be made for all our family's important celebrations – and so, of course, it is the cake I chose to make for Grandma's 100th birthday party. The beauty of this cake is that you can wrap it in foil and freeze it. In hot weather there's not even any need to thaw it – it's perfect served straight from the freezer.

My family &
other animals

144

Ingredients

8 eggwhites, at room temperature
2 cups sugar
2 teaspoons vanilla extract
4 cups finely chopped cashew nuts

Butter cream

4 cups sugar
8 egg yolks, at room temperature
500 g butter, chopped into
  small chunks
1 tablespoon vanilla extract

Method

1 Preheat the oven to 150°C.

2 Using greaseproof paper, cut out the desired shape of the cake (it can be a simple rectangle or a fancier shape like a heart or someone's initials), then use this template to cut out four more identical shapes. Lightly butter each paper template and lay them out on baking trays.

3 Beat the eggwhites in a bowl, gradually adding the sugar and beating between each addition until stiff, shiny peaks form. With a whisk, gently fold in the vanilla and the nuts, taking care not to overmix. Divide this mixture between the paper templates and spread over evenly. Cook for 20 minutes until firm, then remove from the oven and set aside.

4 Meanwhile, to make the butter cream, bring the sugar and 1 cup water to a boil in a saucepan over medium heat, then simmer, stirring occasionally and brushing down the sides of the pan with a wet pastry brush now and then to prevent the syrup burning. The sugar syrup is ready when fine threads form as the mixture drops from a spoon – at this point, remove the pan from the heat.

5 In an electric mixer, beat the egg yolks until thick and pale yellow. With the motor running on the highest setting, gradually pour in the sugar syrup in a thin, steady stream until all the syrup has been incorporated, then leave the mixture in the bowl to cool to room temperature.

6 Start the motor running again on the highest setting and add the butter, chunk by chunk, and the vanilla until incorporated.

7 Spread this butter cream between the layers of cooked meringue, sandwich them together, then cover the top and sides with butter cream as well. Chill until ready to serve.

Serves at least 12

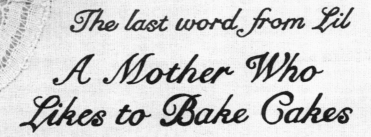

The last word from Lil

A Mother Who
Likes to Bake Cakes

I have never met anyone who can make such artworks out of cakes as my mother Monica can. Yes, there are those who can create an immaculate birthday cake that looks like it should be on the cover of *Vogue*, or those who effortlessly throw together an amazing, unsinkable soufflé. However, the kind of art I'm alluding to is a combination of much thought and planning, immense effort and hours of finicky dedication.

Every cake my mother creates is perfectly suited to the person she has made it for. For my fourth birthday, she made an exact replica of the Emerald City, complete with yellow-brick road. She had stayed up with the mice, baking individual yellow bricks for Dorothy and the scarecrow to walk upon. My brother's first birthday coincided with Easter, and so the Easter Bunny was recreated in sponge – its left ear, which fell off in transit, needed to be cleverly re-attached at the last minute. The year that my great-grandmother turned ninety, not only did Mum cook Sans Rival (see previous page), cheesecakes and rumballs, but she slaved away to produce ninety individual petits fours, finishing them just as the guests began to arrive. It was unfortunate that one of the guests brought their large and rather hungry whippet and allowed him to get a bit too close to the dessert table, leading to the loss of a few sugar-violetted cakes.

But there can be a downside to this unbridled creativity. My dear mama has completed some of her most spectacular cakes just moments before we were due to depart for the occasion, which can be problematic. A word from the wise – iced cakes often need time to set. To those who do wish to ice their masterpiece, make sure the cake has cooled completely (obvious, yes, but when time is short, such seemingly insignificant details can easily be overlooked). If you are transporting the cake in a car, ensure the cake sits firmly

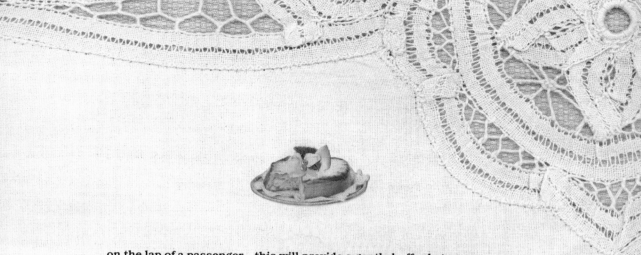

on the lap of a passenger – this will provide a gentle buffer between the cake and the floor on sharp corners. (However, best to tell your passenger not to wear silk as the inevitable spilled icing will most definitely stain.) If you're in a zippy two-door hatchback, the cake gets priority in the front seat, but be sure to take a tea towel and a small bag of extra icing, as touch-ups may be required. In cases of complete icing collapse, flowers will make any cake look divine and can cover up any disasters. 'Travelling with cakes' used to be the bane of Julian's existence, although he couldn't deny that each and every one of Mum's cakes was a masterpiece.

All these successes and disasters have certainly left their mark on me. When my dear friend Mahalia was turning 21, I offered, in my excitement, to bake the cake. This led to two days spent making Rev Bev's famous refrigerator cake, stacked in three towers and covered in chocolate-dipped cherries, biscotti and some judiciously placed flowers. Then the whole edifice was slapped on the unsuspecting lap of my friend Loki as we drove frantically to Balmain. Although we were almost up-ended by an unmarked speed hump, the cherries stayed in place and the cake remained on the dish, although Loki did have to change his shirt due to the cream stains.

But the best attempt was made by none other than Julian, who, for Monica's 23rd birthday, decided to make a huge set of red lips. Coming in at half a metre long and almost as wide, the chocolate-flavoured concoction was covered in incredibly sugary icing that had copious amounts of red food dye added. Unfortunately, the colour that resulted was more reminiscent of Tina Turner than of my dear sweet mama.

May you enjoy all the cakes you bake, and always remember to make them with love.

acknowledgements

Had anyone told me that writing a cookbook would be equivalent to giving birth to an elephant (that is, an extraordinary challenge with a two-year gestation period), I would never have believed them. I like to think of myself as an optimist, but there were moments when even I doubted this project would ever end! To all those courageous people who came on the safari with me and pushed me through to the final oasis, I offer my deepest gratitude.

First to the beautiful Meredith Gaston, or 'Meredici' as I have renamed her, who is responsible for the whimsical watercolours that appear in this compendium of love and madness. I am thrilled to have her illustrations dancing through this book.

My warmest thanks to the Penguin team at Surry Hills. To publisher Julie Gibbs, who had the foresight and generosity to let me run wild with bits of felt, lace and lunacy; I trust her eyes with my vision, and her heart with my family history. Also to Ingrid Ohlsson, for her gentle advice and encouragement. To Virginia Birch, my lovely, patient editor and guardian angel, thank you for every word and query, and for the effort you have put into making the endless recipes readable – I hope you pass this book on to your daughter with love and pride. To Evi O., the magical designer, whose imagination and determination to pull this book together with wit and integrity was tireless. To the unassuming but wise and wonderful senior designer Daniel New, whose attention to detail I cherish, and to Tracey Jarrett in Production who 'whisked' the book into its final state. The 'Penguini' family, as I refer to them, are watched over by the charming Melissa Day at reception, who nurtured me with good coffee and a sunny nature, and always made my visits delightful. I couldn't have wished for a more harmonious, enthusiastic environment in which to create my first book.

A big thank you to my Reclaim family, who ran the shop with such dedication during the creation of this book, including the Riley sisters, Hannah and Elisa, and their generous-spirited mum, Julie; the elegant Michael Garner, whose loyalty and spontaneity knows no bounds; and Simone Holst, whose enviable knowledge of food I tap into frequently and whose wicked sense of humour keeps me buoyant.

I would never have been able to tackle this book and all my other projects without the support of Jodie Pryor, the kind, brave woman who has been responsible for organising my professional life for the last eighteen years. I also thank my literary agents, Lisa Hanrahan and Mark Byrne, for introducing me to Penguin.

To my family, both 'new' and 'old', thank you for putting up with the chaos, the culinary experiments, the mess in the office and my exhaustion. To my parents, thank you for your courage, and to my siblings, I love you for all that you've taught me. To my sons Atticus and 'Olwah', who care for me unconditionally and encourage even my worst cooking disasters, and to my daughters Lil, Phoebe, Georgia and Victoria, for whom I wrote this book – I hope you will all become accomplished cooks and pass on the family secrets to your daughters. And a very special thanks to my aunt Jenny Esteban for all the beautiful black and white photographs that she has kindly allowed me to use.

Lastly, but most importantly, to the love of my life, Simon, who after the two years of pandemonium it took to write this book, still married me . . .

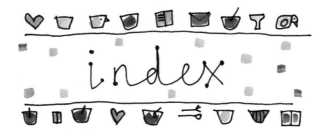

index

LANTERN

Published by the Penguin Group
Penguin Group (Australia)
250 Camberwell Road, Camberwell, Victoria 3124, Australia
(a division of Pearson Australia Group Pty Ltd)
Penguin Group (USA) Inc.
375 Hudson Street, New York, New York 10014, USA
Penguin Group (Canada)
90 Eglinton Avenue East, Suite 700, Toronto, Canada ON M4P 2Y3
(a division of Pearson Penguin Canada Inc.)
Penguin Books Ltd
80 Strand, London WC2R 0RL England
Penguin Ireland
25 St Stephen's Green, Dublin 2, Ireland
(a division of Penguin Books Ltd)
Penguin Books India Pvt Ltd
11 Community Centre, Panchsheel Park, New Delhi – 110 017, India
Penguin Group (NZ)
67 Apollo Drive, Rosedale, North Shore 0632, New Zealand
(a division of Pearson New Zealand Ltd)
Penguin Books (South Africa) (Pty) Ltd
24 Sturdee Avenue, Rosebank, Johannesburg 2196, South Africa

Penguin Books Ltd, Registered Offices: 80 Strand, London, WC2R 0RL, England

First published by Penguin Group (Australia), 2009

1 3 5 7 9 10 8 6 4 2

Text and collages copyright © Monica Trápaga 2009
Illustrations copyright © Meredith Gaston 2009

The moral right of the author has been asserted

Design by Evi O. © Penguin Group (Australia)
Cover and internal collages by Monica Trápaga
Cover and internal illustrations by Meredith Gaston
Author photograph by Richard Birch
Typeset in ITC Bookman by Post Pre-Press Group, Brisbane, Queensland
Colour reproduction by Splitting Image, Clayton, Victoria
Printed and bound in China by 1010 Printing International Limited

National Library of Australia
Cataloguing-in-Publication data:

Trápaga, Monica.
She's leaving home / Monica Trápaga.
9781921382062
Includes index.
Cookery.

641.5

penguin.com.au/lantern